Contexts in Literature

Writing Lives:
Literary Biography

Midge Gillies

Series editor: Adrian Barlow

CAMBRIDGE
UNIVERSITY PRESS

CAMBRIDGE UNIVERSITY PRESS

Cambridge, New York, Melbourne, Madrid, Cape Town, Singapore, São Paulo, Delhi

Cambridge University Press
The Edinburgh Building, Cambridge CB2 8RU, UK

www.cambridge.org
Information on this title: www.cambridge.org/9780521732314

First published 2009

Printed in the United Kingdom at the University Press, Cambridge

A catalogue record for this publication is available from the British Library

ISBN 978-0-521-73231-4 paperback

Editorial management: Gill Stacey

Cover illustration: 'A.L. Kennedy's Writing Room', Copyright Eamonn
McCabe 2007.

Contents

Introduction

Today we know an awful lot about the lives of our bestselling writers. Publishers demand that authors give readings, agree to be interviewed by journalists, attend literary festivals and write articles for newspapers and magazines. Most books include, at the very least, a few biographical details about the author – even if it is no more than a list of their previous works. Many writers, or their fans, have their own websites; some also write a 'blog' to help readers follow their working lives.

Such is the celebrity status of a few authors that they can make headlines beyond the literary pages of newspapers and magazines. The revelation that Ian McEwan had a long-lost brother was reported in many broadsheet newspapers, only a few weeks after claims that he had used phrases from a nurse's memoir of the Second World War in his novel, *Atonement*. Arundhati Roy's opposition to the Narmada Dam in India was widely reported and public burnings of Salman Rushdie's *The Satanic Verses* stayed in the public eye for months. Newspapers recorded that Iris Murdoch's brain had been donated for medical research and reports that scientists were studying how Alzheimer's might have affected the language she used in her last novel raised fascinating questions for anyone interested in her work.

There is nothing new in the desire to know about the lives of famous authors and to speculate about how their life experiences may have influenced their work. What has changed over time is the way in which literary lives are portrayed, from the writer's own account in an autobiography, letters or journal to an outsider's version in the form of a literary biography.

Writing Lives aims to explore those changes, and the cultural and historical factors that have driven those changes. It examines how biography has evolved from Plutarch in the 1st and 2nd centuries to writers such as Doctor Johnson and James Bosworth in the 18th century. The book considers the conventions in different historical periods and the biographers who overturned or questioned those conventions. In what ways, for example, was Mrs Gaskell in the 19th century as groundbreaking as Lytton Strachey in the 20th?

While literary biography is at the heart of the book, *Writing Lives* also looks at autobiographies, journals and letter writing – each of which have their own stand-alone literary merits, as well as being vital tools for the biographer. This range of material should help the student to appreciate the sources available to the biographer and how they can be interpreted in different ways.

The texts chosen and referred to are primarily by English language writers, although they include writers from a wide range of nationalities, as most of the issues and moral dilemmas surrounding life writing transcend language. Many of the extracts are taken from texts that may be hard to find; others have been chosen to encourage the student to read the text in its entirety.

Writing Lives sheds light on the biographer's way of working and the choices they face when using the material they have gathered. The book aims to make the reader more critically aware of how life writing is created and the different forms it can take. It also poses questions about how life writing may evolve in future.

Biography, perhaps more than other genres, carries a moral imperative and *Writing Lives* encourages the reader to make up their own mind about whether that imperative has been met or transgressed. Oscar Wilde was clear where the biographer stood. In *The Critic as Artist* (1891) he wrote: 'Every great man nowadays has his disciples, and it is always Judas who writes the biography.'

Why are writers so wary of the biographer and should readers be just as sceptical? What did the biographer, Peter Ackroyd, mean when he said, 'Every biography is a prisoner of its time' and what are the factors that might affect the biographer's approach to their subject? Is the reader on safer ground if they listen only to the autobiographical writings of the author?

This book will explore what exactly is meant by 'life writing' and look at the advantages and dangers of using it to interpret an author's work. It will examine the areas where biography and fiction overlap and look at more recent developments in the genre. *Writing Lives* will provide an historical background to life writing but, with a few notable exceptions, focus mainly on texts written in the 19th century and later. The book aims to encourage students to revisit familiar texts armed with a deeper sense of the context in which the author wrote and to read new work with a fresh eye.

How this book is organised

Part 1: Reading life writing
Part 1 gives a chronological survey of life writing, stressing how different cultural approaches are used in different historical periods.

Part 2: Approaching the texts
This part examines the different forms of life writing and the challenge of writing about them in different contexts.

Part 3: Texts and extracts
Part 3 provides a range of extracts from life writing and other texts to illustrate points made in the book and to provide a focus for tasks and assignments.

Part 4: Critical approaches
This part explores the different ways that critics have responded to *Alfred and Emily* by Doris Lessing and other examples of her life writing.

Part 5: How to write about life writing
Part 5 considers the task of writing about different forms of life writing, and the different responses it can produce.

Part 6: Resources
This part contains a chronology of texts and writers discussed, together with guidance on further reading, and a glossary and index. (Terms which appear in the glossary are highlighted in bold type when they first appear in the main text.)

At different points throughout this book, and at the ends of Parts 1, 2, 4 and 5, there are tasks and assignments, designed to help the reader reflect on ideas discussed in the text. Where reference to a poem or prose extracts is followed by a page reference, the passage will be found in this book, usually in Part 3: Texts and extracts.

1 | Reading life writing

- What is life writing?

- Which biographers are important?

- What ideas and conventions affect the writing of biography?

- How do autobiography and autobiographical fiction differ from biography?

Modern biography

Richard Holmes, who made his name with a mould-breaking life of Shelley, marks the beginning of his career as a professional biographer from the day his bank bounced a cheque that he had inadvertently dated '1772'. Most biographers would identify with this immersion, so deep that it makes the past seem more real than the present.

Holmes' approach to biography is literally to follow in his subject's footsteps: to sit where Shelley sat when he composed his poems, to camp where Robert Louis Stevenson camped while he was writing *Travels with a Donkey in the Cévennes*. Other biographers – even deeply scholarly ones – talk of being 'haunted' by their subject, so that they feel they are being nudged by them in a certain direction from beyond the grave.

Writing a biography is a huge commitment. Michael Holroyd took nearly ten years to complete his life of Lytton Strachey and this is not an unusually long period. The **literary biographer** is searching for clues and evidence from an author or poet's life that will illuminate their work. How did Virginia Woolf's relationship with her parents affect the way she wrote her novels and to what extent are some of her characters reflections of them? How did living through the First World War and the Spanish Civil War mould her views on pacifism? As part of their search, biographers must immerse themselves in the subject's writing, their life history and the times in which they lived.

Biographers can become so obsessed with their task that they unwittingly adopt the speech patterns of their subject or go to extreme lengths to verify a footnote. Several writers of fiction have used this phenomenon as a central theme of their novels. A.S. Byatt in *Possession: A Romance* and Carol Shields in *Mary Swann* both examine the obsession of the literary biographer, while Julian Barnes' *Flaubert's Parrot* looks at how difficult it can be to pin down even the most banal facts associated with a writer.

But biography is only part of the picture. The biographer – and reader – can learn much about an author and their work from a whole range of writing that includes autobiography, memoirs, journals, letters and autobiographical fiction, poetry and non-fiction. This often tangled web of versions of the same story is frequently referred to as life writing. Hermione Lee, for example, has described Virginia Woolf's essay, *A Room of One's Own*, as a 'disguised economic autobiography' because it draws on her personal experience as a girl who missed out on university when family funds were used to educate her brothers. The essay is just one clue to Woolf's life; her novels, diaries, journalism and letters provide others, as do similar sources from people who knew her – friends, family, colleagues, fellow authors. Life writing is never about just one life.

Sources

As well as the range of sources, the biographer may also face a huge difference in the *number* of documents he or she can consult. Anyone writing about Shakespeare will have very few indisputable facts to play with. Even his date of birth is open to question – was it 23 April, or the day before? George Bernard Shaw, by comparison, wrote ten letters every day of his adult life. When Michael Holroyd was researching his life, he began to feel that Shaw, who had shorthand and secretaries at his disposal, could write more in a day than Holroyd could read.

The biographer may have to contend with family and friends who are keen to protect the reputation of a writer, either by drip-feeding the release of documents such as diaries or journals or by allowing limited use of work still in copyright. Worse still, from the biographer's point of view, is the deliberate destruction of letters or other vital documents. The smell of burning **primary sources** lingers over the story of many literary biographies. Charles Dickens made two big bonfires of his papers and committed a multiple offence by hurling correspondence from Tennyson, Thackeray and Wilkie Collins into the flames. Thomas Hardy, Henry James and Samuel Johnson each burnt papers that biographers would have loved to have got their hands on, and Mary Taylor destroyed a cache of letters from her friend, Charlotte Brontë.

Modern biographers are a particularly nosy bunch, driven to examine a writer's private life in the greatest of details. No peccadillo or private eccentricity remains unexposed in the search for insight into a writer's work. Victorian biographers, by comparison, mainly sought to present sanitised lives that confirmed their own moral code. Many great writers have had their foibles tucked away from view by 19th-century biographers, only for later biographers to expose them to public glare.

Much of the excitement for the modern biographer – and his or her reader – is the detective work used to unmask the true author. Take for example, *Queen Mab*, widely regarded as Shelley's first major poem. Never fully satisfied with the work, he continued to tinker with it – even after publication. Today it is possible to glimpse something of Shelley's creative process in the trail of corrections he made in his own handwriting in a first edition that he left with his landlord in Marlow. The book had several subsequent owners, including the forger H. Buxton Forman and the composer Jerome Kern, until Carl Pforzheimer bought it for his collection (now owned by the New York Public Library). The poem, together with various scribblings and sketches, can be seen at: www.nypl.org/research/chss/spe/rbk/mab. html or in *Shelley and His Circle*, vol. IV, pages 514–568.

Whether the biographer faces a tottering pile of documents or a few scraps of paper, each presents dilemmas of what to include and what to leave out. As Hermione Lee, whose subjects include Virginia Woolf, Edith Wharton and Willa Cather, says, 'Biography is a process of making up, or making over.' How biographers approach their sources will depend on many factors, including their own personal interests and the age in which they are writing and its preoccupations.

▶ Draw up a list of your favourite writers. What do you know about each and where does that information come from? How reliable is each source? Does your knowledge of the author affect the way you read their work? Have you ever been surprised by something you've read about a writer?

The influence of early biographers

Plutarch

Greek and Roman writers such as Xenophon, Suetonius, Tacitus and Pliny were the first to show an interest in life writing and to provide a model for early English biographers. Plutarch's *The Lives of the Noble Grecians and Romans* was particularly influential.

Plutarch (*c.* 50–125 AD) was born in Chaeronea in Greece. He studied mathematics and philosophy in Athens. As an adult he held municipal posts and ran a school which specialised in ethics and philosophy. He was also a priest at the temple of Apollo at Delphi. Although he was proud of his Greek heritage, he respected the Roman imperial system and was well connected within its highest echelons; he may even have known the emperors Trajan and Hadrian.

He is thought to have written as many as two hundred and twenty-seven works: *Moralia* (moral essays), essays on politics and a series of parallel biographies – probably written towards the end of his life. In *Lives* Plutarch teams up pairs of public figures, such as soldiers and politicians – one Roman, one Greek – whose characters and careers are similar. Although modern editions usually divide *Lives* into two series, Plutarch viewed each pair, such as Dion, the soldier and intermittent ruler of Syracuse (at that time part of the Greek empire), and Brutus, the politician who plotted against Julius Caesar, or Alexander and Caesar, as one entity. Typically, each begins with an introduction explaining why they have been placed together. The biographies follow, usually the Greek first, and end with a comparison.

Plutarch draws on a range of sources, some of them unashamedly gossipy, and, unlike previous histories, his approach is warm and often anecdotal. As he says in 'Alexander':

> I am not writing history but biography, and the most outstanding exploits do not always have the property of revealing the goodness or badness of the agent; often in fact, a casual action, the odd phrase, or a jest reveals character better than battles involving the loss of thousands upon thousands of lives, huge troop movements, and whole cities besieged … I must be allowed to devote more time to those aspects which indicate a person's mind and to use these to portray the life of each of my subjects.
>
> (from the introduction to *Roman Lives*, Oxford World Classics)

He uses sources that the modern biographer would instantly recognise: letters, public documents, conversations with friends. Plutarch's readers are expected to find the *Lives* morally uplifting as they assess the choices taken by each subject.

Plutarch influenced several centuries of thinkers including the French writer and philosopher Jean-Jacques Rousseau (1712–1778) and the German thinker Friedrich Nietzsche (1844–1900). The poet John Dryden, who edited a new translation of *Lives*, first published in 1683–1686, praised him for revealing the home lives of great men. But by the early 19th century Plutarch's influence had started to slip as the **Romantic Movement** placed greater emphasis on passion, rather than control. However, Plutarch's parallel biographies and range of sources anticipate the modern biographer's preoccupation with a new way of presenting a life.

▶ Look at the extract from Plutarch (Part 3, page 97). From this piece what attributes would you say were important to Plutarch?

Shakespeare and the *Lives*

Sir Thomas North translated the *Lives* into English in 1579, and Shakespeare drew heavily on it as an historical source for his Roman plays and as inspiration for other works. Richard Field, who was at school with Shakespeare, published a revised edition in 1595 and James Shapiro, a 21st-century biographer of Shakespeare, believes that Shakespeare 'thumbed through a copy' searching for names to use in *A Midsummer Night's Dream*: 'By late 1598 he had begun to read the *Lives* in earnest.' In his book *1599: A Year in the Life of William Shakespeare* (2006), Shapiro argues that Plutarch's influence is evident in *Henry the Fifth* – not only in the way in which Henry is compared to another great soldier, Alexander the Great, but, much more importantly, in Shakespeare's efforts to convey the interior life of his characters.

Shapiro describes how in 1599 the playwright 'buried' himself in North's translation when planning *Julius Caesar*, rather than using the Roman historian, Tacitus (AD 56–*c*.120). Shapiro points out the risk that Shakespeare was taking in tackling the subject of political assassination at a time when Elizabeth I faced many threats from at home and abroad:

> At the same time, his choice of working through Plutarch – who had been largely overlooked as a source by London's professional playwrights – was a careful and canny one. He knew, as did everyone else who was within earshot of the court, that Queen Elizabeth herself had been absorbed in translating Plutarch ('On Curiosity') just a few months earlier. Even as Tacitus leaned towards republicanism, Plutarch was at heart a monarchist. And, it's worth noting, Shakespeare named his play after Caesar (who only appears in a few scenes, and except for his ghost is gone midway through the play), rather than Brutus, hero to republicans, who occupies centre-stage throughout.
> (from *1599*)

Izaak Walton and the Restoration

Izaak Walton (1593–1683) was strongly influenced by Plutarch and his eagerness to stress the positive aspects of his subjects' lives. Walton is best remembered for his book on the joys and tactics of fishing, *The Compleat Angler* (1653), but he also wrote five biographies – mainly of clerics.

Although Walton received little formal education, he read widely and developed intellectual interests, fostered through his friendships with men such as John Donne who was vicar of a church close to where Walton lived in London and who shared his love of fishing. Walton wrote 'An Elegie' to accompany a posthumous collection of Donne's poetry and a biographical piece for inclusion in a book of Donne's sermons that he later revised and enlarged.

Walton's sympathy for the Royalist cause and his religious beliefs are reflected in his choice of subjects. He wrote biographies of the provost of Eton, Sir Henry Wotton; the Elizabethan theologian, Richard Hooker; the poet George Herbert and Bishop Sanderson. He also responded to requests for information from John Aubrey who was researching the lives of the famous. Here, for instance, Aubrey inserts a comment from Walton about the playwright Ben Jonson (1572/3–1637):

> My Lord of Winton told me, he told him he was (in his long retyrement, and sicknes, when he saw him, which was often) much aflickted, that hee had profain'd the Scripture, in his playes; and lamented it with horror; yet, that at that time of his long retyrement, his pentions (so much as came yn) was given to a woman

that govern'd him, with whome he livd and dyed nere the Abie in
Westminster; and that nether he nor she tooke much care fore next
weike, and wood be sure not to want Wine; of which he usually tooke
too much before he went to bed, if not oftner and soner.

(from *Brief Lives* by John Aubrey)

▶ Can you detect evidence of Walton's own sympathies in this extract?

John Aubrey

Both Walton and Aubrey (1626–1697) were writing at a time of great political
and religious turmoil, and it may have been the destruction of so many historical
artefacts and the transformation of institutions – most obviously the monarchy
and church – that compelled them to record history that might otherwise have
been lost.

Like Walton, Aubrey was extremely well-connected. He had struck up
friendships at Trinity College, Oxford and while studying law at the Middle
Temple; he also had useful family connections. Today he might be described as
a 'good networker', a talent that proved extremely useful when his father's debts
and various lawsuits left him penniless and reliant on the hospitality of friends.
His friendship with men such as the 17th-century architect, Sir Christopher
Wren, and the philosopher Thomas Hobbes were also helpful when he started to
collaborate with the reclusive antiquarian, Anthony Wood, who was working on
a history of Oxford University. This *History* was later developed into *Athenae et
Fasti Oxonienses*, a hybrid of biography and bibliography, which was published in
1691–1692.

Aubrey's research went far beyond Wood's remit and resulted in biographical
sketches of some of the leading men – and a few women – of his age that were
eventually deposited in the Ashmolean Museum in Oxford. These sketches
remained largely unknown until 1761 when a scholar spotted their reference to
poets including Shakespeare and Milton. The first selection of what was to become
known as *Brief Lives* was published in 1813 but it was not until 1898 that an
accurate transcript of Aubrey's manuscripts appeared. Even then, this edition failed
to acknowledge that Aubrey's apparently haphazard structure was in fact following
a format prescribed for the *Athenae*. His occasional bawdiness (as in this extract
from the life of Sir Walter Raleigh) also failed to endear him to Victorian editors
who **bowdlerised** his work.

He loved a wench well: and one time getting-up one of the Maids
of Honour against a tree in a Wood, who seemed at first boarding
to be something fearfull of her honour, and modest, cryed, 'Sweet
Sir Walter what doe you meane? Will you undoe me? Nay sweet Sir
Walter! Sweet Sir Walter: Sir Walter!'

WRITING LIVES

Aubrey's later reputation was dented by his interest in the supernatural: the only book published in his lifetime was *Miscellanies* (1696), a collection of papers on the occult. In his defence, he lived at a time when interest in magic still had a legitimate place on the scientific spectrum and he was one of the original fellows of the Royal Society, founded in 1660 for the study of science.

He gathered information for *Brief Lives* from a range of sources, including public monuments, pamphlets and written requests from people who knew his subjects. He left a trail of notes revealing his particular system of working. Ellipses (…) show a piece of information was either unknown or had already been printed and he cites sources (for example, 'Vide [see] Memorandum') or 'quaere' [enquire] or 'quaere plus de hoc' if something should be checked or expanded. So, for example, Milton is about the same height as the author but this requires the qualification: 'Quaere quot [how many] feet I am high; response, of middle stature.' He suggests who to approach for verification and in some cases the subjects themselves check the material. *Brief Lives* is not without errors – Sir Edward Shirburne, for example, wrongly states that it was Ben Jonson who killed fellow playwright Christopher Marlowe, rather than the actor Spencer.

Aubrey's eclectic interests, including archaeology, folklore, astrology and whether it was possible to read a person's character by their physiognomy, helped him to write vivid, intimate descriptions. Milton's complexion, for example, was 'so faire, they called him the Lady of Christ's-college'. Aubrey's use of anecdote foreshadows the stylistic approach of James Boswell (1740–1795), although he is much more concise than Boswell. His first hand accounts put the reader within touching distance of some of the greatest writers in the English language.

▶ Read the extract from Aubrey's life of Shakespeare (Part 3, page 78). What advantage did Aubrey have over modern biographers and how is this demonstrated in the extract? How do his style and his attitude to sources compare with other biographical extracts in Part 3?

The biographer as friend

Samuel Johnson

Today Dr Samuel Johnson (1709–1784) is most often remembered for two things: his Dictionary, which was published in 1755, and his friendship with the Scottish lawyer and writer, James Boswell (1740–1795) which led to the publication of *The Life of Samuel Johnson* in 1791, a work frequently claimed as the first great biography. But Johnson contributed as much to the **genre** as a biographer as he did as a biographical subject.

His *An Account of the Life of Mr Richard Savage, Son of the Earl Rivers* was published in 1744, while Johnson was a penniless and struggling writer. Indeed, it was this state of destitution which drew him to his subject, who had fallen on equally hard times. Much of the inspiration and material for Johnson's subsequent biography were gleaned from night-time walks around London with his poet friend, when both were too poor to take refuge at an inn. While later biographers tried to follow in the footsteps of their subject, Johnson and Savage walked side by side.

At first glance the two seem very different. Savage was in his forties (his date of birth was one of several disputed facts about him) when he first met Johnson, who was twenty-nine. Savage claimed to be the illegitimate son of the late Earl Rivers and Countess Macclesfield and spent much of his life fighting for his birthright. Johnson was a schoolmaster who had left his wife at home in Lichfield, in the Midlands, to try to make his literary name in London. He was awkward in company, scarred by childhood scrofula and prone to depression. Savage, by comparison, was witty and dashing and very good at extracting money from his literary patrons. He had been convicted of killing a man in a brothel near Charing Cross – for which he received a royal pardon – and published a bestselling poem, 'The Bastard', in 1728.

When Savage died in a debtors' prison in Bristol in 1743, Johnson, who had already written several short biographical essays, immediately decided to write a biography of his friend. He announced publicly that he would defend Savage's reputation and his partisanship is clear from the start of his biography:

> To these mournful narratives, I am about to add the life of Richard Savage, a man whose writings entitle him to an eminent rank in the classes of learning, and whose misfortunes claim a degree of compassion, not always due to the unhappy, as they were often the consequences of the crime of others, rather than his own.
>
> (from *Johnson on Savage*, ed. Richard Holmes, *Classic Biographies* series, 2002)

The book, which ran to forty-five thousand words, was Johnson's first full-length biography and his first about a contemporary subject. It was also, in many ways, a 'first' in the history of biography. Although Johnson is clearly sympathetic to Savage's plight, his account breaks away from the **tradition** of pious medieval **hagiographies**. And, unlike Boswell's biography and William Godwin's memoir (1798) of his wife, Mary Wollstonecraft (author of *A Vindication of the Rights of Woman*), Johnson avoids giving himself a prominent part in the narrative.

Richard Holmes, in his book *Dr Johnson and Mr Savage* (1993), says that Johnson's life of Savage made it possible for the biographer to

> … take obscure, failed and damaged lives, and make them intensely moving and revealing. Biography was an act of imaginative friendship, and depended on moral intelligence and human sympathy. Biography had become a new kind of narrative about the mysteries of the human heart.

Johnson's penetrating psychological insights went much deeper than anything offered by 17th-century writers of biographical compilations or his contemporaries' preference for tittle-tattle and anecdote. His approach has a greater dramatic range and depth than previous biographies and draws on Savage's poetry, essays and letters in a way that helps to make the book more authoritative. Although it would be anachronistic to suggest that the stress Johnson puts on Savage's childhood and adolescence is **Freudian**, he is nevertheless the first biographer to attempt a psychological assessment of his subject.

The book's immediate and huge success helped Johnson to secure a generous advance for his *Dictionary*. Although he did not attempt another biography like *Savage*, he defended his approach in three essays. In 'On the Dignity and Usefulness of Biography' (*The Rambler* No 60, 1750) he argues for the importance of a psychological understanding of the biographical subject, saying:

> More knowledge may be gained of a man's real character, by a short conversation with one of his servants, than from a formal and studied narrative, begun with his pedigree, and ended with his funeral.
>
> (from *Johnson on Savage, Classic Biographies*)

James Boswell

Johnson and James Boswell offer another unlikely pairing. As a young adult Boswell spent much of his time trying to escape the plans laid down for him by his strict Scottish father, a lawyer and landowner who wanted his son to follow his own profession. Boswell tried many careers, but liked best the coffee house culture of London where he could be rowdy and lascivious. He was also a compulsive journal keeper.

He had already started to make copious and detailed notes about Johnson before he eventually met him on 16 May 1763. Johnson was thirty-one years his senior and famously anti-Scottish. After an initial coolness they became firm friends, and met frequently over the next few years when Boswell visited London and when they travelled together in the Hebrides (the subject of a book published in 1785). Boswell used their meetings to interview his friend, although he was too busy with other subjects to start writing a biography. Boswell published his first successful book, about Corsica, in 1768, but it seems that it was not until 1775 that he began to talk seriously about a biography.

It was only when Johnson died in 1784 and Boswell was asked to prepare a book of his quotations that he realised that this would not do him justice. He began work on a biography, supplementing his own journal notes with interviews from people who had known Johnson. It was an agonisingly slow process, during which time Boswell had the irritation of seeing – as so often happens when a famous person dies – a clutch of rival biographies appear ahead of his, including one by another close friend of Johnson's, Mrs Henry Thrale (later Mrs Piozzi).

Boswell's biography in 1791 was not given anything more than favourable reviews until 1831, when both Thomas Macaulay and Thomas Carlyle wrote enthusiastically about the book's vivid portrayal of 18th-century life. Since then it has been recognised as a landmark in biography – indeed, probably the first great biography.

Detractors have criticised Boswell for his failure to tell the truth about elements of Johnson's life, most notably his marriage to Tetty, a much older widow, his relationships with other women, his tendency to eat and drink to excess and his sometimes coarse language. Boswell has been accused of inflating his relationship with Johnson as a way of furthering his own literary ambitions. Certainly, they spent much less time together than Boswell would like his reader to think and they did not meet until Johnson was fifty-three. Another legitimate criticism is that Boswell's biography is skewed towards the last twenty years of Johnson's life and is excessively long.

But what sets the biography apart is Boswell's depiction of Johnson's inner, depressive self, as counterbalanced by the liveliness of his life in the tavern and coffee house. The tension between the two gives the book a novelistic depth and an insight into the human condition.

Victorian biography: the biographer as guardian

Like Boswell and Johnson before them, several Victorian biographers chose close friends as their subjects. John Forster (1812–1876) wrote a three-volume biography of Charles Dickens who made him his literary executor. Thomas Carlyle (1795–1881) produced a life of his close friend, John Sterling (1806–1844) and James Froude (1818–1894) startled readers with his frank description of the Carlyles' unhappy marriage in his biographies of the author.

But the *Dictionary of National Biography* (*DNB*), which was first published in 1885, is more typical of the Victorian approach to biography, with its emphasis on the public lives of great men. Sir Leslie Stephen was its first editor and his daughter, Virginia Woolf, later wrote of the 'draperies and decencies' of Victorian biography that it represented ('New Biography', 30 October 1927, *New York Herald Tribune*).

Victorian biographies were usually monuments to virtue in which any doubts about a subject's morality were airbrushed out of the narrative. The families and friends of writers such as Jane Austen, Percy Bysshe Shelley and Charles Dickens, for example, jealously guarded their reputation. These guardians of a particular image only released material they felt was in keeping with a preconceived image and made it available only to a vetted biographer; to avoid the wrong impression many sources were simply destroyed.

Several aspects of Shelley's life did not fit well with Victorian sensibilities, particularly his exile, the way he turned his back on his social class, his subversive beliefs and his sexual proclivities. His father shielded readers from such details by preventing anything from being written until after his own death and, in particular, by denying Shelley's second wife, Mary, a chance to present her version of his life. When Shelley's father died, Lady Jane Shelley (Shelley's daugher-in-law) 'made it her life work to establish an unimpeachable feminine and Victorian idealisation of the poet' (Richard Holmes). She tidied away details that failed to fit in with the image of the heroic poet, such as Shelley's abandonment of his first wife, Harriet, and her suicide when heavily pregnant.

For a discussion of the myths surrounding Shelley's death by drowning, at the age of twenty-nine, see: books.guardian.co.uk/review/story/0,12084,1129144,00. html

Jane Austen's family kept an even tighter hold on their famous writer. Long after Jane's death in 1817 any biographical account was a family affair. The first was written by her brother, Henry Austen, and took the form of a 'Biographical Note' in the 1818 edition of *Northanger Abbey* and *Persuasion*. Nieces, a nephew and more distant relatives added their own testimony, each stressing her sweet disposition. In a chapter on her character in his memoir of 1870 her nephew, James Edward Austen-Leigh, described how much children liked her and how good she was with her fingers, whether folding and sealing envelopes or working with a needle. In the chapter on her death he stressed her religious beliefs and modesty.

> She was a humble, believing Christian. Her life had been passed in the performance of home duties, and the cultivation of domestic affections, without any self-seeking or craving after applause. She had always sought, as it were by instinct, to promote the happiness of all who came within her influence, and doubtless she had her reward in the peace of mind which was granted her in her last days. Her sweetness of temper never failed. She was ever considerate and grateful to those who attended on her.

This image of a life passed without passion persisted well into the early 20th century.

Mrs Gaskell and Charlotte Brontë

Charlotte Brontë, probably more than any other author, is associated with the main character of her major work. Indeed, the book's full title, *Jane Eyre: An Autobiography* appears to court this comparison. Her friend and posthumous biographer, Mrs Gaskell, saw it as her duty to rescue Charlotte Brontë from herself and to explain to the world what had caused her to produce such a passionate novel.

When Charlotte wrote her story of the governess who falls in love with her employer, Mr Rochester, but cannot marry him because he already has a wife – the insane Bertha who is kept locked in the attic – she was determined to keep her identity hidden from her neighbours in Yorkshire, which forms the bleak backdrop of her story. Charlotte and her sisters Emily and Anne had already published a book of poetry under the **pseudonyms** Currer, Ellis and Acton Bell in 1846. Charlotte's second novel, *Jane Eyre*, Emily's *Wuthering Heights* and Anne's *Agnes Grey* were all published the following year. But it was Charlotte's passionate story and the raw emotion of the first-person narration that caused an immediate literary sensation. The mystery surrounding the author's identity, and whether he had also written *Wuthering Heights* and *The Tenant of Wildfell Hall*, fuelled interest in *Jane Eyre*, until Charlotte and Anne visited London to set the record straight. But by then, as rumours spread that the authors were female, critics started to attack the novels' 'coarseness': the use of slang and biblical **allusions** and the books' violence and passion. Probably most damning was an anonymous article in the *Quarterly Review* of December 1848 that described the character of Jane Eyre as an affront to the accepted image of women. The novel was unchristian and – the article implied – Currer Bell must be a fallen woman.

Mrs Gaskell had long taken an interest in Charlotte, and had formed a strong impression about her and her life before they met for the first time in 1850. Another four meetings followed and they exchanged letters until Charlotte's death in 1855 when her father, Patrick, asked Mrs Gaskell to write a life that would correct the version produced by 'the great many scribblers' who were attacking the Brontës. Mrs Gaskell set out to present a life of suffering that would explain and exonerate any coarseness in Charlotte's writings. Here she describes a scene from her early life:

> Into the midst of this lawless, yet not unkindly population, Mr Brontë brought his wife and six little children, in February, 1820. There are those yet alive who remember seven heavily-laden carts lumbering slowly up the long stone street, bearing the 'new parson's' household goods to his future abode.
>
> One wonders how the bleak aspect of her new home – the low, oblong, stone parsonage, high up, yet with a still higher background of sweeping moors – struck on the gentle, delicate wife, whose health even then was failing.

The world Mrs Gaskell created (see Part 3, page 86) – of the lonely parsonage at Haworth set on the isolated moors, the unstable father who banned his daughters from proper learning and Charlotte's controlling husband who ended her writing career – was in several important respects entirely false. Haworth was not as remote or as bleak as Mrs Gaskell made out and Charlotte read newspapers and journals that kept her well informed about national politics. Mrs Gaskell's tales of Charlotte's father, Patrick, burning hearth rugs and sawing up chairs are second-hand accounts from a servant who was sacked from the Brontë household; there is no evidence that their father did not encourage his daughters' education. Neither is it fair to claim that marriage stopped Charlotte from writing. She had only been married a few months when she died and was, indeed, working on a new book.

Mrs Gaskell was also guilty of sins of omission, most notably the evidence – which she chose to overlook – that Charlotte had been in love with her Belgian tutor, Constantin Heger. Not only were there letters to support this theory but the infatuation is revealingly close to Lucy Snowe's love for Paul Emanuel in *Villette*. Her first, unpublished novel, *The Professor*, obviously contains parallels with Heger.

Despite these oversights, Mrs Gaskell's style was in many ways revolutionary. She showed her subject in an intimate light – Charlotte cutting the black bits out of potatoes that had been missed by her blind servant – and quoted extensively from letters (see Part 3, page 86) in a way that had not been done before. But Mrs Gaskell's own skills as an author made her biography so compelling that her description of the lonely vicarage became the dominant image associated with the Brontë sisters. It was to be over a century before biographers managed to challenge Mrs Gaskell's portrayal of inspiration born purely of misery.

▶ Look at the extract from Mrs Gaskell's *Life of Charlotte Brontë* (Part 3, page 86). What sort of picture does Mrs Gaskell paint of daily life at Haworth? How would you describe the personality of Charlotte Brontë that emerges in this extract?

Bloomsbury: experiments in biography

While Mrs Gaskell chose a subject who was not a typically Victorian public figure, Sir Edmund Gosse selected a bastion of 19th-century society, but then wrote a complete reappraisal seventeen years later. In 1890 he published his first life of his father, the zoologist and strict Christian Philip Henry Gosse. After this conventional version an alternative, *Father and Son*, appeared in 1907 and proved a devastating and moving portrayal seen from the child's viewpoint. In subverting the established form Gosse was anticipating the next major development in biography.

Lytton Strachey

From the perspective of the 21st century it is easy to underestimate just how startlingly different *Eminent Victorians* appeared to its readers. The book was published on 9 May 1918 when the country had been at war for four years. Its author, Lytton Strachey (1880–1932), was a well-known conscientious objector and lifelong friend of Virginia Woolf's. While he was working on the essays that make up *Eminent Victorians*, Woolf and other members of the **Bloomsbury Group** acted as critics as the work evolved over several years.

Strachey's publisher, Chatto & Windus, announced the book would take 'a new view' of Cardinal Manning, Florence Nightingale, General Gordon and Doctor Arnold, headmaster of Rugby School. The choice of subjects was as significant as Strachey's revolutionary approach to biography. Together the three men and one woman represented the central planks of Victorian Britain: church, self-conscious do-gooding, imperialism and the public school system. Strachey's 'attack' landed on a war-weary readership. As Strachey's biographer, Michael Holroyd, says in his Introduction to *Eminent Victorians,* 'Evangelicism, liberalism, humanitarianism, education, imperialism – these were Strachey's targets, and he struck them beautifully.'

Soon after its publication, *The Times* called *Eminent Victorians* 'brilliant and extraordinarily witty' and *The Sunday Times* called it 'audaciously amusing'. In a lecture at Oxford University on 'Aspects of the Victorian Age', Herbert Asquith argued that Strachey had approached his subjects 'not in the blind spirit of hero worship' but using a 'subtle and suggestive art'. In the late 20th century the academic Paula Backscheider, in *Reflections on Biography,* described Strachey's work as being inscribed with 'the impact of Freud, the cynicism and disillusionment of the First World War generation, and a particular kind of pervading scepticism characteristic of **Modernism**'.

▶ To what extent does the following extract from *Eminent Victorians*, in which Strachey describes the end of Florence Nightingale's life, demonstrate the biographer's 'subtle and suggestive art'?

> Looking back, she was amazed by the enormous change which, since her early days, had come over the whole treatment of illness, the whole conception of public and domestic health – a change in which, she knew, she had played her part. One of her Indian admirers, the Aga Khan, came to visit her. She expatiated on the marvellous advances she had lived to see in the management of hospitals, in drainage, in ventilation, in sanitary work of every kind. There was a pause; and then, 'Do you think you are improving?' asked the Aga Khan. She was a little taken about, and said, 'What do you mean by 'improving'?' He replied, 'Believing more in God.' She saw that he had a view of God which was different from hers. 'A most interesting man,' she noted after the interview; 'but you could never teach him sanitation.'

Strachey followed *Eminent Victorians* with a biography of Queen Victoria – a choice levelled directly at the central figure of an age, but which was affectionate, if irreverent. In *Elizabeth and Essex: A Tragic History* his focus on Elizabeth I's relationship with her father suggested a Freudian interpretation of her treatment of her favourite courtier.

Virginia Woolf

'Life writing' is a term that Virginia Woolf 'all but coined', according to one leading biographer and critic (Kathryn Hughes, *Guardian*, 29 December 2007). Woolf grew up surrounded by biography. As well as editing the *Dictionary of National Biography* her father, Sir Leslie Stephen, wrote almost four hundred entries himself and produced lives of well-known writers. Privately, he wrote a memoir of his dead wife for her children, which the family referred to as his *Mausoleum Book*.

His daughter left behind a huge legacy of life writing that continued to expand after her death, as her husband, Leonard Woolf, gradually released editions of her writing. Her life can be read in several different ways: through her letters (many written to other members of the Bloomsbury Group); through her five volumes of diaries; through her essays and lectures on feminist themes, most famously *A Room of One's Own*; through her novels, which draw heavily on her own experiences; or through her imaginative adventures in biography: the fantastical, gender-switching *Orlando*, inspired by her close friend, Vita Sackville-West, which included spoof acknowledgements; and the playful biography of Elizabeth Barrett Browning's spaniel, *Flush*. Her biography of the painter Roger Fry was, by comparison, more conventional.

Woolf shared Strachey's interest in exposing the stultifying effect of Victorianism, but her view of biography is much more complex than his. Strachey dedicated *Queen Victoria* to Woolf and she claimed the book would change the way people viewed the monarch. However, she loathed Strachey's *Elizabeth and Essex*.

Virginia Woolf – diaries

Her friendship with Strachey, and other members of the Bloomsbury Group, is one reason why Virginia Woolf's diaries, which first started to appear in published form in 1977, are so compelling. Like any diary they do not always tell the whole truth, but they shed light on her approach to writing and on other significant influences such as her friendships and the state of her mental health. As her biographer Hermione Lee says, 'Her diary, like her essays and stories and novels, blurs the lines between history, biography and fiction.'

The diaries also allow the reader to piece together the minutiae of Woolf's life, such as worries about servants, wartime rationing and concerns about her appearance. Although these details may seem frivolous – and modern writers have poked fun at some of the more banal entries in her diary – they help to build up a detailed picture of what her life was really like.

Woolf used nicknames for many of her acquaintances and anyone researching her life must decode these to make sense of the diaries and letters. She calls her friend, Emma Vaughan, for example, 'Toad', and when writing to Vita Sackville-West refers to herself as 'Bosman's potto' (an African lemur) and Vita as 'Dolphin' or 'Donkey'. In her marriage to Leonard Woolf ,Virginia was his 'ugly monkey' or 'mandril', while he was her 'mongoose'.

A year and a half after completing *To the Lighthouse*, a diary entry for 28 November 1928 appears to explain what had driven her to write the novel.

> 1928
> Father's birthday. He would have been 1832 96, yes,
>   96
> today; & could have been 96, like other people one has known; but
> mercifully was not. His life would have entirely ended mine. What
> would have happened? No writing, no books; – inconceivable. I used
> to think of him & mother daily; but writing The Lighthouse, laid them
> in my mind. And now he comes back sometimes, but differently.
> (I believe this to be true – that I was obsessed by them both,
> unhealthily; & writing of them was a necessary act.) He comes back
> now more as a contemporary. I must read him some day. I wonder if I
> can feel again, I hear his voice, I know this by heart?

Woolf's diaries and letters are also significant because of the literary circle in which she moved. Her reputation as a radically new writer, together with the Hogarth Press which she ran with her husband, Leonard, and her connections with the Bloomsbury Group allowed her to meet some of the most influential writers of her day. She frequently commented on them in her diary and letters. In June 1922, for example, T.S. Eliot came to dinner at her home, Hogarth House and read from his new poem, *The Waste Land*. She recorded her impressions in her diary entry for 23 June:

> He sang it & chanted it rhythmed it. It has great beauty & force of
> phrase: symmetry; & tensity. What connects it together, I'm not
> so sure … One was left, however, with some strong emotion. The
> Waste Land, it is called; & Mary Hutch, who has heard it more quietly,
> interprets it to be Tom's autobiography – a melancholy one.

▶ Look at the two extracts from Woolf's diaries, Monday 14 March and Tuesday 20 September 1927 (Part 3, page 103). How does her diary style compare with her way of writing fiction? What do the two entries tell us about the development of an idea – in this instance, *Orlando*?

Virginia Woolf – letters

Like most writers of her time, Virginia Woolf spent much of her day composing letters and these began to be published in 1975. Some deal with apparently mundane matters, such as hiring a servant or developments at the Hogarth Press. Each has the possibility to shed light on her life and work.

In the extracts below she is writing to her close friend, Vita Sackville-West. They met in 1922 when Sackville-West was the more successful writer and before she had secured her modern-day fame for her garden at Sissinghurst and the stately home of Knole. At the time that she was becoming intimate with Woolf, Sackville-West had an 'open marriage' with the diplomat, Harold Nicolson, and travelled widely with him.

Here she writes to Woolf on her way to Persia (modern-day Iran) on 23 February 1926:

> Why is it that critics pay so little attention to style and surface-texture? It is the last thing you ever see mentioned, whether for good or evil. Either you go in for style or else you don't; the Russians apparently don't, judging by the translation which I somehow feel reproduces pretty exactly the manner of the original; but if you do, then I think you ought to get credit for it. Now you ... have the *mot juste* more than any modern writer I know ... The funny thing is, that you are the only person I have ever known properly who was aloof from the more vulgarly jolly sides of life. And I wonder whether you lose or gain? I fancy that you gain, – *you*, Virginia, – because you are so constituted and have a sufficient fund of excitement within yourself, though I don't fancy it would be to the advantage of anybody else. I feel with Proust, '*Il faut avoir passé par là*' [literally, 'you would have needed to pass that way']. You will say you have. But not in precisely the way I mean ...
>
> (from *The Letters of Vita Sackville-West to Virginia Woolf*, edited by Louise DeSalvo and Mitchell Leaska)

Woolf replies on 16 March 1926 when she is in the throes of writing her novel, *To the Lighthouse*.

> As for the *mot juste*, you are quite wrong. Style is a very simple matter, it is all rhythm. Once you get that, you can't use the wrong words. But on the other hand here am I sitting after half the morning, crammed with ideas, and visions, and so on, and can't dislodge them, for lack of the right rhythm. Now this is very profound, what rhythm is, and goes far deeper than words. A sight, an emotion, creates this wave in the mind, long before it makes words to fit it; and in writing (such is my present belief) one has to recapture this, and set this working (which has nothing apparently to do with words) and then, as it breaks and tumbles in the mind, it makes words to fit it: But no doubt I shall think differently next year. Then there's my character (you see how egotistic I am, for I answer only questions that are about myself) I agree about the lack of jolly vulgarity. But then think how I was brought up! No school; mooning about alone among my father's books; never any chance to pick up all that goes on in schools

... This is an excuse: I am often conscious of the lack of jolly vulgarity but did Proust pass that way? Did you? ...

▶ In what ways does this exchange give you a different insight into Woolf's writing from the entries quoted above (page 24)?

Virginia Woolf – autobiographical fiction

'Fiction is often her version of biography', Hermione Lee writes (*Virginia Woolf*) before going on to explain the complex relationship between Woolf's life and her works of fiction.

On one level it is easy to guess where inspiration may have come from. *Orlando* is in some ways based on her friendship with Vita Sackville-West and *Mrs Dalloway* may represent something of her own marriage – or her relationship with London. Lee believes that when, in 1905, Virginia and her siblings return to linger outside Talland House, near St Ives, where they spent many happy summers as a family, the visit provides the inspiration for *To the Lighthouse* and that the house also appears in her earlier novel, *Jacob's Room*.

But if the ingredients of her novels can be traced directly to specific events, people or places, the end result is overlaid with so many themes that the novel is much more than a collection of autobiographical references. *Mrs Dalloway*, for example, also addresses the futility of war and the pervading class divisions that continued to thrive after it.

Woolf's own view appears in a letter to fellow novelist Hugh Walpole:

... and then because as you know, of all literature (Yes, I think this is more or less true) I love autobiography most.
  In fact I sometimes think only autobiography is literature – novels are what we peel off, and come at last to the core, which is only you or me.   (*Letters*, 28 December, 1932)

▶ The above quotation raises as many questions as it answers. What do you think Woolf means by 'the core'?

Early autobiography: Margery Kempe

With a few exceptions, autobiography is a relatively recent form of writing. 'Memoir' and 'autobiography' are often used interchangeably, but traditionally a memoir relies less on facts and more on remembered events and impressions. An autobiography or biography usually takes a chronological approach to someone's life, whereas a memoir often focuses on one theme or period of that life.

The *Book of Margery Kempe*, which is believed to have been dictated in the 1420s, is an example of a very early form of autobiography. It may even be the first ever autobiography in the English language.

Margery Kempe (c.1373–1439) grew up in Norfolk where her father was mayor of King's Lynn. She married John Kempe, but abandoned her marriage after twenty years and fourteen children to devote herself to a life of piety. She made pilgrimages to Jerusalem, Rome, Compostela in Spain and Wilsnack in Poland. Her book includes accounts of these travels.

She also describes her religious visions in a way similar to Julian of Norwich (c.1342– after 1416) who was one of the first female authors to write in English. Julian was a recluse who lived in a cell next to the church of St Julian at Norwich and wrote *A Book of Showings* and *Sixteen Revelations of Divine Love*.

Both women dictated their thoughts, which were transcribed in the **vernacular**, and both followed a tradition of personal narrative used to explore a spiritual journey. But the *Book of Margery Kempe* is much more than a mystical text. Although Kempe refers to herself remotely as 'this creature', her forceful and sensual personality nevertheless emerges in the story of her trial for heresy, her struggle with madness (possibly a form of postnatal depression) and her battle against lecherous temptations. But, as one commentator has said, Kempe's autobiographical approach is more ordered than might at first appear:

> The book's apparent spontaneity has a kind of charm, but it is a beguiling spontaneity, for beneath the apparent disorder there is a kind of logic – a thematic logic dictating the ordering of events within the narrative.
>
> (from *The Book of Margery Kempe: The First Autobiography in English?* by Lucy Lewis, in *Women's Autobiographical Writing*)

Modern autobiography

Examples of autobiography are rare until the 20th century when the influence of Freud and an emphasis on introspection provided a climate conducive to such writings.

The experience of war produced the impetus for many of the most powerful autobiographies of the last century. In *Goodbye to All That* (1929) Robert Graves, the poet and author of historical novels such as *I, Claudius*, described, among other subjects, his unhappy childhood and the failure of his first marriage. However, the autobiography is most often remembered as an 'anti-war book' because of the way Graves portrays his experiences of the trenches and how they shaped his later life.

Testament of Youth (1933) by Vera Brittain (1893–1970) reflects the author's strong belief in pacifism, feminism and the need for social change. She describes growing up as the daughter of a wealthy paper manufacturer from Newcastle-under-Lyme, Staffordshire in the North Midlands, and her struggle as a woman to obtain an equal education. But *Testament of Youth* has remained popular because of its personal and deeply moving account of the First World War. Brittain was twenty-one years old when war was declared and abandoned her studies at Somerville College, Oxford to enrol as a volunteer nurse. She witnessed at first hand the horrors of the Western Front and experienced the unimaginable pain of losing not only her fiancé, Roland Leighton, and her brother, Edward, but two close friends. Brittain wrote two further volumes of autobiography: *Testament of Friendship* (1940), about her friend, Winifred Holtby, and *Testament of Experience* (1957).

▶ Look at the extracts in Part 3 (pages 82–86). One is taken from a letter to her brother, Edward; the other is from *Testament of Youth*. Both describe the same event – Brittain visiting Roland's home on the day that his belongings were returned to his family. Which facts and quotations from the letter has the author chosen to use in her published work and which has she omitted? What might have influenced her decision? How are the styles in each extract different? Which do you think is the more powerful piece of writing?

Painstaking research by Mark Bostridge who, together with Paul Berry, wrote *Vera Brittain: A Life* (2001) uncovered evidence that Brittain's brother Edward may have been homosexual. Bostridge concluded that Edward may have shot himself, or deliberately put himself in mortal danger during the battle in which he was killed in order to avoid a court-martial for involvement in homosexual relationships with men in his company.

▶ How, if at all, does this revelation affect our understanding of Vera Brittain's life and of the experience of a First World War soldier?

Life writing and the Second World War

As with any intense and painful experience, the Second World War produced a wealth of life writing, including diaries, letters and memoirs. Several novels written after the war were based on the authors' experiences of conflict. Captivity, whether as a member of the armed forces or as a civilian, proved an inspiration for others.

The Holocaust: *The Diary of Anne Frank*

The Nazis' mass murder of Jews during the Second World War became the subject of a wide range of literature – much of it life writing. Accounts of the Holocaust were not immediately popular, but the publication of Anne Frank's diary (which appeared in English in 1952 under the title, *The Diary of a Young Girl*) provoked interest in the subject that has continued to grow. The diary, which she started to write on her thirteenth birthday, has been translated into over sixty languages and is one of the most widely read books in the world.

Anne was born in Germany but moved to the Netherlands to try to escape the

Nazi persecution of Jews. After the German invasion of Holland she hid with her family and four others in the attic of a house in Amsterdam. Here she wrote her diary (in Dutch), addressing her thoughts to an imaginary friend, 'Kitty'. The final entry appeared on August 1, 1944, three days before she was arrested. She died of typhus, aged fifteen, in Belsen concentration camp. Her father was the only member of her family to survive and published his daughter's diary in 1947. The writings provide an intimate account of life in hiding, as well as an insight into their author's hopes for the future, and have become a literary memorial to the tragedy of the Holocaust.

The following two extracts show how, on one hand, Anne was an ordinary teenager experiencing the usual ambivalent feelings towards her parents (although, of course, that tension was exacerbated by extraordinary conditions), while on a different level she was caught in a terrible tragedy that affected a whole people.

Dear Kitty,   Saturday, 3 October, 1942

Yesterday Mother and I had another run-in and she really kicked up a fuss. She told Daddy all my sins and started to cry, which made me cry too, and I already had such an awful headache. I finally told Daddy that I love 'him' more than I do Mother, to which he replied that it was just a passing phase, but I don't think so. I simply can't stand Mother, and I have to force myself not to snap at her all the time, and to stay calm, when I'd rather slap her across the face. I don't know why I've taken such a terrible dislike to her. Daddy says that if Mother isn't feeling well or has a headache, I should volunteer to help her, but I'm not going to because I don't love her and don't enjoy doing it. I can imagine Mother dying someday, but Daddy's death seems inconceivable. It's very mean of me, but that's how I feel. I hope Mother will *never* read this or anything else I've written.

Dearest Kitty,   Friday, 9 October 1942

Today I have nothing but dismal and depressing news to report. Our many Jewish friends and acquaintances are being taken away in droves. The Gestapo is treating them very roughly and transporting them in cattle-trucks to Westerbork, the big camp in Drenthe to which they're sending all the Jews. Miep told us about someone who'd managed to escape from there. It must be terrible in Westerbork. The people get almost nothing to eat, much less to drink, as water is available only one hour a day, and there's only one lavatory and sink for several thousand people. Men and women sleep in the same room, and women and children often have their heads shaved. Escape is almost impossible; many people look Jewish, and they're branded by their shorn heads.

If it's that bad in Holland, what must it be like in those faraway and uncivilised places where the Germans are sending them? We assume that most of them are being murdered. The English radio says they're being gassed. Perhaps that's the quickest way to die.

For more about Anne Frank, her hiding place and her writings see the Anne Frank Museum in Amsterdam: www.annefrank.org

The Holocaust: Primo Levi

Whereas Anne Frank's diaries provide a testament to the millions whose lives were cut short by the Holocaust, the autobiographical work of Primo Levi (1919–1987) offers not only an insight into life in the concentration camp at Auschwitz but an examination of how victims dealt with the legacy of their survival and wider issues about humanity.

Levi was born in Turin, Italy and studied chemistry at university. In 1943 he joined a partisan group in northern Italy fighting against the Fascists, but was caught and taken to Auschwitz concentration camp. Here his knowledge of science provided a lifeline as the Nazis forced him to use his expertise to help them make synthetic rubber. Levi was ill with scarlet fever when the Germans left Auschwitz in January 1945, taking with them 20,000 prisoners, who subsequently vanished. Levi, left behind, survived.

▶ The Irish teacher Brian Keenan was taken hostage in Beirut, Lebanon in 1986 and held for four years. Look at the extract from his memoir, *An Evil Cradling* (Part 3, page 87), in which he describes the unexpected treat of being given an orange to eat. Compare this extract with Primo Levi's description of his own gnawing hunger (page 91).

After the war Levi returned to Italy where he worked as an industrial chemist and managed a paint factory. He wrote about his experiences of captivity in *If This is a Man*, which was published in October 1947. Initially it sold only about 1500 copies. He followed this with *The Truce* about his return journey from Auschwitz and *The Periodic Table* which blends autobiography with philosophy. Levi also wrote two novels, poetry and short stories.

In a review of Ian Thomson's biography, *Primo Levi, A Life* (2002), Anthony Grafton described Levi as:

> The creator of a genre of his own – a cross between the story and the essay, neither pure memoir nor pure fiction – Levi brought a clear eye; a pure, lean prose; and an amazingly judicious habit of mind to bear on the *anus mundi*, Auschwitz, where he had learned that he and everyone else inhabited a gray zone in which the violence of captors and fellow prisoners alike leached away character and morality.
>
> (*The New York Times*, 8 November 2003)

Levi's quiet, studied approach to his experience owed much to his training as a scientist; he was also able to imbue his work with a humour and tolerance that few other concentration camp survivors could muster. At the time of Levi's death Philip Roth, the American novelist, described how Levi had 'set out systematically to remember the German hell on earth, steadfastly to think it through, and then to render it comprehensible in lucid, unpretentious prose. He was profoundly in touch with the minutest workings of the most endearing human events and with the most contemptible.' (*The New York Times*, 12 April 1987)

Primo Levi died in 1987, falling down the stairwell at the block of flats in which he lived and where he had been born. His death was assumed to have been suicide: although there was no suicide note, friends reported that Levi had been suffering from a depression that had several roots – not all of them connected to the Holocaust. For some readers Levi's suicide altered their view of his writing. Since his books had always offered hope and an understanding of inexplicably horrific events, did his suicide make his writings suddenly hopeless? Did his suicide mean the Nazis had won?

▶ Carole Angier's biography of Primo Levi appeared in the same year as Ian Thomson's (2002). Both writers had to address the fact and possible causes of Levi's suicide. In what ways do you think a biographer approaching the subject of a living author might face different challenges from a biographer writing about a dead writer?

Women's autobiographical writing

Mass Observation

For centuries women have chosen to record their thoughts in diaries or journals or through letters to friends and families. In most cases these records have remained private and unpublished, but some have found wider audiences. Many women discovered an outlet for their private thoughts by writing for Mass Observation, an organisation set up in 1937 by anthropologist Tom Harrisson, poet Charles Madge and film-maker Humphrey Jennings. Their aim was to create an 'anthropology of ourselves', and they recruited a panel of observers and diarists to record everyday life around Britain. These volunteers were promised anonymity, but many of their accounts have since been published using pseudonyms – either in anthologies or in volumes devoted to one diarist. Perhaps the most well known is *Nella Last's War: The Second World War Diaries of Housewife, 49*, which was made into a television drama. *Can Any Mother Help Me?* is a collection of letters uncovered by a researcher in the Mass Observation Archives. The letters were written between women who set up a private magazine, 'The Cooperative Correspondence Club', as a vehicle for them to share their problems and which lasted for fifty-five years.

Mass Observation provided an outlet for ordinary people to write about their lives with a startling frankness, as in this extract from the diary of Nella Last, written on Christmas Day, 1943, when food such as sweets could only be bought using coupons:

I said 'Happy Christmas' to my husband. He scowled and muttered. I looked at him. I thought, 'Over thirty-two years of *slavery*, patience beyond belief, your house kept a home, whatever happens, your meals ready always, perfectly cooked and served – yet I'm treated with less consideration than the average man would dare to treat a servant. Not a flower, a card – or a sweet, although you had the sweet coupons in your pocket, thereby preventing me from getting any myself.' I felt as if a little flickering flame burned even lower.

Several writers of fiction have mined the Mass Observation archives for inspiration and to give their writing authenticity. Andrea Levy consulted the collection for her novel, *Small Island* (2004), which won the Orange Prize for Fiction, the Whitbread Book of the Year and the Commonwealth Writer's prize. The novel examines the experiences of two Jamaican immigrants to Britain: Gilbert, who served in the RAF during the war, and his new wife, Hortense.

The novel also contains a strong autobiographical core. Levy was born in England to parents who had emigrated from Jamaica in 1948. Her father was among some five hundred men who sailed on the *Empire Windrush* from the Caribbean to start a new life in Britain. As a child she remembers her parents talking about the white people who took them in and how they reacted to the immigrants. One of the themes in her novel is the ways in which an established population reacts to outsiders.

Levy spent four and a half years writing the book and has said that one of the reasons why it took so long was the amount of research she did. As well as using Mass Observation, she interviewed men who had served in the Second World War and she read newspapers from the period:

Sometimes I would spend days researching something only to realise nothing of that research would actually appear in the book – it was just that I had to know and understand the information.

(*Daily Telegraph*, 28 May 2004)

The novel has four narrators: Hortense, Gilbert, their landlady Queenie Bligh and her husband Bernard. Each has a very distinctive voice. Hortense and Gilbert have a prickly relationship, but as the novel progresses reach something close to a truce. Here Hortense chides her husband for criticising what she is wearing:

The silly carefree countenance slipped from his face with such force it bump on to the floor. He make me feel sorry for the words.

His bottom lip protruding with their harshness. His eye displaying sorrow. I thought to apologise for that quick tongue. But then he start cussing – sucking on his teeth, and cha, cha, chat on me like a ruffian. So I paid him no mind.

Ah, even the sun was shining. Only a weak light but enough to raise my spirits higher than this stupid man's worry. My two letters of recommendation each contained words that would open up the doors of any school to me. Despite the slow start at the school for scoundrels in Half Way Tree, my headmaster had seen fit to call my teaching skills proficient. Looking for the meaning of the word in the English dictionary. I was honoured to see he thought me expert …

▶ In the extract above how does Andrea Levy create Hortense's voice and what does this piece reveal about her character? How does the style compare to that of another first person narrator in Maya Angelou's *I Know Why The Caged Bird Sings* (Part 3, page 76)?

Sylvia Plath

It is impossible to read the work of poet and novelist Sylvia Plath (1932–1963) without being conscious of at least the best-known facts of her life and death – her marriage to Ted Hughes (1930–1998), who would later become Poet Laureate, and her suicide. However, many other aspects of her life had an influence on her work. She was born in Boston, Massachusetts and her father, a German immigrant professor, died suddenly of undiagnosed diabetes following a leg amputation when she was eight. The memory of his death and of surgery haunt her poems.

Plath was a highly competitive, but troubled, student. In the summer of 1953 she won a competition to spend a month in New York, working on the fashion magazine *Mademoiselle*. That same year she attempted suicide when she was at college and was given Electro Convulsive Shock Treatment (ECT), a controversial treatment for depression. She won a Fulbright Fellowship to study at Newnham College, Cambridge where she met Hughes. He was the son of a carpenter from West Yorkshire where he had become fascinated by the violence and beauty of nature, themes that re-occur in his poetry.

They married in 1956, but their relationship was sometimes tempestuous. They spent a year teaching in America before moving to London, and then retreating to a rural life in Devon where Plath, like her father before her, kept bees. Hughes initially had greater success as a published poet and Plath's first volume of poetry, *The Colossus*, did not appear until 1960.

They had two children, Frieda and Nicholas, before eventually separating in late 1962. Plath committed suicide in a London flat by putting her head in a gas oven after protectively sealing the rooms where her children slept and leaving them bread and milk. A collection of her poems, *Ariel*, was published in 1965. It was dedicated to her children.

Plath started to keep a diary when she was a child and continued until just before her suicide. The journal reveals her doubt in herself and the conflict she felt between her different roles: as teacher, writer, wife, mother. This extract was written in September 1951 when she was studying at Smith College in Massachusetts:

> So I am led to one or two choices! Can I write? Will I write if I practice enough? How much should I sacrifice to writing anyway, before I find out if I'm any good? Above all, CAN A SELFISH EGOCENTRIC JEALOUS AND UNIMAGINATIVE FEMALE WRITE A DAMN THING WORTHWHILE? Should I sublimate (my, how we throw words around!) my selfishness in serving other people – through social or other such work? Would I then become more sensitive to other people and their problems? Would I be able to write honestly then of other beings besides a tall, introspective adolescent girl? I must be in contact with a wide variety of lives if I am not to become submerged in the routine of my own economic strata and class. I will *not* have my range of acquaintances circumscribed by my mate's profession. Yet I see that this will happen if I do not have an outlet … of some sort.
>
> (from *The Journals of Sylvia Plath*, 1982)

▶ Compare this extract with Virginia Woolf's diary (page 24, above, and in Part 3, page 103). How does the style of their diary entries differ? Are there any outside influences that might explain some of these differences?

Two notebooks containing Plath's journals from late 1959 to within three days of her death have not survived. One disappeared and Hughes destroyed the other to spare his children, commenting later, in the foreword to the 1982 edition of her journals: 'in those days I regarded forgetfulness as an essential part of survival'. Hughes also comments that nearly all her earlier writings suffered from her ambition to see her work published and 'to produce what the market seemed to require'. But, he argues, her journals are different:

> Here she set down her day-to-day struggle with her warring selves, for herself only. This is her autobiography, far from complete, but complex and accurate, where she strove to see herself honestly and fought her way through the unmaking and remaking of herself. And the Sylvia Plath we can divine here is the closest we can now get to the real person in her daily life.

Plath's work is clearly strongly autobiographical. Her only novel, *The Bell Jar* (1963), opens in New York in 1953 when Julius and Ethel Rosenberg are executed for spying for the Soviet Union. The narrator is Esther Greenwood, a highly ambitious young woman from Boston who spends time working for a woman's magazine. When she returns home she has a breakdown and is given ECT. But there is a danger that the tragic elements of Plath's life – her mental illness, the tortured relationship with Hughes and her suicide – have overshadowed the joy which drives many of her poems, for example, 'Morning Song' (see Part 3, page 97) – the first poem in *Ariel*.

▶ What might be the downside of knowing *too* much about a writer's life? How hard is it to read the work of Plath and Woolf without placing too much emphasis on the fact of their suicides?

Hughes' collection of poems, *Birthday Letters*, was published in 1998. All but two poems are addressed to Plath. In 'Visit' he remembers as a young man in Cambridge throwing earth at the window that he and his friend believed belonged to Plath:

> Drunk, he was certain it was yours.
> Half as drunk, I did not know he was wrong.
> Nor did I know I was being auditioned
> For the male lead in your drama,
> Miming through the first easy movements
> As if with eyes closed, feeling for the role.
> As if a puppet were being tried on its strings,
> Or a dead frog's legs touched by electrodes.

In 2007 Faber and Faber published *Letters of Ted Hughes* which provided further insights into their relationship and the way both poets worked. For example, in a letter of 19 November 1997 to Jutta and Wolfgang Kaussen, who were preparing a selection of his poems for translation into German, Hughes answers their various queries about his work. One concerned 'puckering amputations' which appears in his poem, 'You hated Spain' in *Birthday Letters* and other collections. He tells them:

> Sylvia dreaded passing the beggars who exposed the healed-up
> ends of amputated limbs. The healed-up end was puckered, like
> lips puckered for a kiss, or a purse mouth, draw-string tightened
> close. Her greatest single terror, maybe, as a single image, was an
> amputated limb, as you will know if you are familiar with her work.
> Her father died of diabetic gangrene – successive amputation of foot,
> lower leg etc.

▶ In what ways does knowledge of Plath's life and of her relationship with Hughes bring a greater appreciation of the extract from 'Visit' (above) and the **imagery** used?

Maya Angelou

I Know Why The Caged Bird Sings (1970) is the first of six volumes of autobiography and describes the author's experience of growing up with her grandmother amid poverty and racial segregation in the American South in the 1930s. Angelou, who is a poet and civil rights campaigner, writes in a style that is often lyrical although she tackles themes of violence and sexual assault, including her rape, aged eight, by her mother's boyfriend and an unplanned pregnancy at the age of sixteen. The subject matter led to the book being banned at various times in some schools in the United States. But Angelou was also the first African–American to have a book on *The New York Times* Paperback Non-fiction Bestseller List for a record number of weeks.

Angelou's autobiography is an important landmark in feminist literature because of its fearless first-person account of issues such as race and poverty. To see just how startling and fresh her approach is compare it with *Cider with Rosie* (1959) by Laurie Lee (1914–1997) in which he describes an idyllic country childhood in the Cotswolds using a style that revels in nature and a nostalgia for a pre-industrial age. *As I Walked Out One Midsummer Morning* (1969) continues the story of his life after leaving home and travelling to Spain, on the eve of the civil war.

Extracts from a BBC interview with the author are available at: www.bbc.co.uk/bbcfour/audiointerviews/profilepages/leel1.shtml

Janet Frame

While Lee's and Angelou's memoirs added to their standing as authors and poets, the literary reputation of the New Zealand writer, Janet Frame (1924–2004), was for a long time overshadowed by critics' knowledge of her life. Frame's earlier years were marked by tragedy: two of her sisters drowned in separate incidents and she endured crippling depression as a result. She was misdiagnosed as suffering from schizophrenia and held in mental institutions for nearly a decade.

Her first book, *The Lagoon And Other Stories*, was published in 1952 and won New Zealand's only literary award. The prize led to the cancellation of a frontal lobotomy which would probably have left her in a vegetative state. After her release Frame's fiction drew heavily on her experience of mental illness and family tragedy. In much the same way that Sylvia Plath's suicide has made an objective assessment of her poetry problematic, so Frame's penetrating insight into the human psyche has led some critics to conclude that only a 'mad woman' could produce such work, rather than recognising her unique literary talent. On several occasions, as a way of countering this label, she brandished a psychiatrist's letter from the Maudsley Hospital in south London, which confirmed that she had never suffered from schizophrenia and was not mentally ill.

The publication of three volumes of autobiography – *To The Is-Land* (1982), *An Angel At My Table* and *The Envoy From Mirror City* (both 1984) – helped to untangle the threads binding her fiction to the events in her life. She herself was unsure about the differences, saying: 'I am not really a writer. I am just someone who is haunted, and I will write the hauntings down' (*Daily Telegraph*, 29 January 2004). Michael Holroyd described the trilogy as 'one of the greatest autobiographies of this century' and Jane Campion's film *An Angel At My Table* (1990) ensured that Frame had a worldwide readership.

Family memoirs

In the second half of the 20th century several authors drew on unorthodox, or unhappy, childhoods to write memoirs that were both entertaining and insightful.

Joseph Randolph Ackerley (1896–1967), more commonly known as J.R. Ackerley, pushed autobiography into new realms of frankness with *My Father and Myself* (1968). Ackerley was literary editor of the BBC's magazine, *The Listener,* and produced comic novels and memoirs. But in *My Father and Myself* he wrote about the discovery that his father was leading a double life in which he was secretly head of two families. Ackerley also described his own affection for his dog and his homosexuality. The book was published after Ackerley's death and his sister set up the Ackerley Prize for autobiography in his memory in 1982. It is now called the Pen/Ackerley Prize.

For a list of winners in recent years see: www.englishpen.org/prizes/pastjrackerleyprizewinners

When playwright and author Alan Bennett won the prize in 2006 for his memoir, *Untold Stories*, he commented:

> I must say that the British Book Awards are somewhat nylon, if not crinoline, whereas this award is undoubtedly tweed … I wonder, if he [Ackerley] had been able to write as freely about his life as one can now, whether he would have written the books he did.

▶ What kind of freedom do you think Bennett is talking about and does such freedom necessarily produce the best writing?

Bad Blood

Previous winners of the Pen/Ackerley Prize include Lorna Sage (1943–2001) for *Bad Blood: A Memoir* (2000), which also won the Whitbread prize for biography, and *And When Did You Last See Your Father?* (1993) by Blake Morrison, the poet and literary critic. Morrison followed this in 2002 with *Things My Mother Never Told Me* in which he revealed the truth about his mother's early life.

Bad Blood tells the story of Sage's childhood in a bleak village on the Welsh borders after the Second World War and in particular her relationship with her grandparents. She inherited her love of books from her grandfather – he named her after *Lorna Doone* by R.D. Blackmore (1869) – and she went on to become a professor of English Literature.

Writing in the *Guardian* on 12 January 2001, just before her death, she explores how a memoir can lead in many directions:

> Starting a memoir, you open a door on to the past. The moment *Bad Blood* became real to me was when, in my mind's eye, I saw just which door, and who was leading the way:
>
> 'Grandfather's skirts would flap in the wind along the churchyard path and I would hang on.'
>
> I am still pleased with the book's first words, though I had no idea what I was letting myself in for. My bitter, theatrical vicar-grandfather, stagnating in the remote rural parish of Hanmer in North Wales for his sins (women and drink, mostly), was my reference point, my black flag on the map of the past, my arrow pointing – 'You were here', this is where you begin.

Memoir and structure

Typically, memoirs are written in chronological order, but British cookery writer Nigel Slater chose an imaginative form through which to tell the story of his childhood. *Toast, The Story of a Boy's Hunger* (2004) is divided up into short sections – often no more than a few pages long. Each section is headed by a title that helps to evoke the 1960s, for example, 'Cold Lamb and Gravy Skin', 'Heinz Sponge Pudding' and 'Butterscotch Angel Delight' (which lists the ingredients in this 'dessert in a sachet').

Food becomes a way of conjuring up the past and the conflicts within his family. Here he describes pickled walnuts in a way that provides an insight into the relationship between his father and his companion, Joan:

> Dad had a taste for odd things I didn't understand. A grey-brown ointment called Gentleman's Relish that he used to spread on triangles of toasted Mother's Pride; Campbell's Meatballs in Gravy; Shippams Chicken Spread sandwiches; Crosse & Blackwell Piccalilli that everyone at school called camel snot; marmalade with whisky in it; porridge with salt instead of sugar; and his precious pickled walnuts – the last sitting in glass jars like anatomical specimens in the damp, dark pantry, tightly sealed against the army of scurrying silverfish that lived under the fridge. 'They're nothing to do with dirt, it's the damp they like,' Joan reminded us every time one made

a break for the skirting board. (The silverfish, that is, not the pickled walnuts.)

One weekend when we attended a fete in a field by the river, Dad came back with a jar of pickled walnuts as big as the jars of sherbet lemons that stood behind the sweet counter in the post office. 'It will last us a year or two,' he said, bringing them in from the boot of the car.

'I don't know how you can eat the filthy things,' shuddered Joan, screwing up her nose like he had just handed her a jar of preserved dog poo.

Misery memoirs

Although *Toast* and *Bad Blood* examine the strains within families, they do so with wit and a sense of exploration – a desire to understand the past, rather than an angry hunt for blame. They are not part of the publishing phenomenon which became known in the late 20th century as 'survivor', or 'misery memoirs'. These books focus on unhappy childhoods, terrible illnesses or abusive relationships; they often end with an act of redemption that sees the authors overcoming tragedy to become successful in their own right.

Dave Pelzer is often cited as the author who launched 'misery memoirs' with his book, *A Child Called It* (1995), which describes in horrific detail a childhood in which his alcoholic mother kept him locked in a basement and subjected him to physical and mental abuse. Later books told of his rescue, his time in foster care and his success as a best-selling author. His first three books have sold more than four million copies in the UK alone.

In *Angela's Ashes* (1996) Frank McCourt recounts a childhood spent in abject poverty in Ireland. The book won the Pulitzer Prize for Biography or Autobiography, although many inhabitants of Limerick claimed not to recognise the town that appeared in McCourt's memoirs. These paragraphs help to set the tone:

When I look back on my childhood I wonder how I survived at all. It was, of course, a miserable childhood: the happy childhood is hardly worth your while. Worse than the ordinary miserable childhood is the miserable Irish childhood, and worse yet is the miserable Irish Catholic childhood.

People everywhere brag and whimper about the woes of their early years, but nothing can compare with the Irish version: the poverty; the shiftless loquacious alcoholic father; the pious defeated mother moaning by the fire; pompous priests; bullying schoolmasters; the English and the terrible things they did to us for eight hundred long years.

Above all – we were wet.

▶ Although McCourt describes an existence that sounds wretched, how does he inject humour into his writing?

Biographical structure and style in the 20th century

Faction

The American writer, Truman Capote (1924–1984), changed the way authors and readers approached non-fiction. Capote, who was born in New Orleans, left school at seventeen and found work on the *New Yorker* and other magazines. He wrote the whimsical *Breakfast at Tiffany's* (1958), several short stories and two novels before turning his attention to a longer work of non-fiction. He was already known in New York literary circles as a flamboyant and attention-seeking writer, but *In Cold Blood* (1966) ensured him a worldwide audience.

The book created a new form – what Capote described as 'the non-fiction novel'. He had wanted to write something radically new for some time and an item in the *The New York Times*, 16 November 1959, provided his starting point.

Wealthy Farmer, three of Family Slain

A wealthy wheat farmer, his wife and their two young children were found shot to death today in their home. They had been killed by shotgun blasts at close range after being bound and gagged. The father, 48-year-old Herbert W. Clutter, was found in the basement with his son, Kenyon, 15. His wife Bonnie, 45, and a daughter, Nancy, 16, were in their beds. There were no signs of a struggle and nothing had been stolen. The telephone lines had been cut. 'This is apparently the case of a psychopathic killer,' Sheriff Earl Robinson said …

With the help of Harper Lee, a childhood friend who was to write *To Kill a Mockingbird* (1960), Capote spent six years researching the brutal murder of the Clutter family in a remote part of Kansas. He interviewed police, local people and even the killers to build up a picture of the murderers, their victims and the night of the killings. Controversially, he did not record his interviews using a tape recorder or notebook because he said this broke the relationship between the interviewer and their subject. Instead, he claimed to be able to memorise whole chunks of speech that he put down in his notebook after the interviews and reproduced in his book.

Capote followed the story through to the execution of the killers. One of the reasons why his approach was so shockingly new was his involvement with the two killers – he became obsessed with the men and built up something close to an affection for them, in particular Perry Smith. In some ways, *In Cold Blood* is as much about Capote as it is about the two murderers. He continued to explore his obsession with the criminal mentality in *Music for Chameleons* (1981), which includes an interview with a psychopathic killer as well his account of attending a funeral with Marilyn Monroe.

Capote said that, before writing *In Cold Blood*:

> I wanted to produce a journalistic novel, something on a large scale that would have the credibility of fact, the immediacy of film, the depth and freedom of prose, and the precision of poetry.
>
> (*The New York Times*, 28 August 1984)

Capote's fiction influenced future writers, particularly those who based their work on, and mingled it with, fact. Thomas Keneally's *Schindler's Ark* (1982), for example, uses documentary evidence about Oskar Schindler, who risked his life to save Jews in Nazi-occupied Poland. The book has been classified as both fiction and non-fiction: in Britain it won the Booker Prize for fiction; in America it was published as non-fiction and retitled *Schindler's List*.

Peter Ackroyd

Many British writers, several of them literary biographers, have used their familiarity with an historical period or person as a basis for fiction. Peter Ackroyd in particular has made a name for himself by blending fact and fiction and by experimenting with biographical form. His novels and his biographies have a strong sense of the past – even if he takes liberties with that past, as he does so often in his biography of Charles Dickens.

Ackroyd was born in East Acton, London, and the capital plays a key role in most of his work; in many of his books it can be viewed as a character in itself. He has even written a biography of the city. His personal associations with London are so strong that it is possible to argue that a strong autobiographical current runs through his work. In a lecture in the 1990s he commented:

> I was brought up on a council estate in west London. It was the very best start in life I could possibly have had because somehow, from an early age, the city became the landscape of my imagination. You don't have to be brought up in a grand house to have a sense of the past, and I truly believe that there are certain people to whom or through whom the territory – the place, the past – speaks.
>
> (quoted in the *Guardian*, 3 July 2004)

In some of his most successful novels Ackroyd introduces famous people into historical settings in London. In *Hawksmoor* he tells the dual stories of the 18th-century architect commissioned to build eight new churches after the Great Fire of London and, two hundred and fifty years later, a detective investigating a series of murders at the churches. *Dan Leno and the Limehouse Golem* is equally sinister and Ackroyd again inserts real-life characters into his fictional confection, including Karl Marx, the writer George Gissing and music hall performer Dan Leno.

He seems always to have enjoyed inventing dialogue for real people – even when they were rather good at it themselves. His second novel, *The Last Testament of Oscar Wilde,* pretends to be an account of the playwright looking back at his life. Critics marvelled at the skill with which Ackroyd appeared to have captured Wilde's voice through aphorisms such as: 'I did not steal lines from other writers. I rescued them … Queensbury had the habit of speaking his mind without realising that he had no mind to speak of.' (quoted in the *Guardian,* 3 July 2004)

Not all critics were so impressed when Ackroyd invented dialogue for Charles Dickens in his monumental biography which appeared in 1990. Ackroyd was said to have secured an advance of £650,000 for a two-book deal to write *Dickens* and a biography of the poet William Blake. At the time, the figure represented a huge amount and helped to establish biography as a genre that carried commercial clout with publishers and booksellers.

As well as inventing dialogue, Ackroyd inserts himself into his biography of Dickens, which runs to over a thousand pages. On one occasion the biographer meets his subject on a train in Essex; in another instance they are together in the Mid-Victorian Room of the Geffrye Museum in the East End of London. (See the extract in Part 3, page 75.)

Ackroyd plays games with the facts in a total of seven diversions: he allows Dickens to enter his own novels and to encounter Little Dorrit; in another diversion various Dickensian characters are placed in the same scene. In one section, entitled 'A true conversation between imagined selves', Ackroyd writes dialogue between T.S. Eliot, the poet Thomas Chatterton (1752–1770), Wilde and Dickens – each of whom Ackroyd has written about. A final section is a question-and-answer dialogue between Ackroyd and an anonymous interviewer. One question he poses is 'But no doubt you will seem wrong-headed in thirty or forty years' time.' Ackroyd responds:

> Every biography is a prisoner of its time, yes, and I'm sure that anyone who may happen to open the book in the twenty-first century will recognise at once that it was written in the fin-de-siècle of the twentieth century …

▶ When Dickens comments to Ackroyd in the museum, 'Oh, biographers. Biographers are simply novelists without imagination!' do you think Ackroyd is relying on the reader to have some knowledge of Ackroyd's other work? Do you think there is a place for these imaginative interludes? Do you think they might be irritating or in some way devalue the biography?

Claire Tomalin: hidden lives

During the first half of the 20th century most biographies were written by and about men. Claire Tomalin helped to change this with her reinterpretations of several literary figures and her discovery of hidden lives.

Tomalin became a biographer relatively late in her career. Her first subject was Mary Wollstonecraft (1759–1797), the English radical who wrote *A Vindication of the Rights of Woman* (1792) in which she argued for equal education for women and other rights which would, much later, be acknowledged as standard feminist doctrine. Tomalin's biography grew out of an article she wrote for the *New Statesman* magazine about Wollstonecraft's love letters which she had discovered in the London Library. After the article appeared several publishers and agents urged her to write Wollstonecraft's biography. The result was *The Life and Death of Mary Wollstonecraft* (1974) which won the Whitbread First Book Prize.

Tomalin's emergence as a biographer coincided with the rise of feminism and her biographies show great sympathy for women struggling against outside forces – whether that takes the form of sexual or social prejudice, as with the actress, Dora Jordan *(Mrs Jordan's Profession*, 1994*)* or, as in the case of the short story writer Katherine Mansfield (1888–1923), illness. Clearly some of this empathy stems from her own life experiences. In a review of Janet Malcolm's biography of Sylvia Plath, who was three years below Tomalin at Cambridge, Tomalin says her most vivid memory of the 1950s 'is of crying into a washbasin full of soapy grey baby clothes', while her husband played football with their friends in the park. 'I thought I had some capacities, and here they were going down the plughole with the soapsuds' (quoted in the *Guardian*, Saturday November 18, 2006).

Claire Tomalin is as much a social historian as a biographer and her early books attempt to shed light on her subjects' daily lives. What was it like for Jane Austen, an unmarried daughter, to write her novels in a bustling, noisy, crowded family house? How did it feel to be a young Victorian actress wearing a boy's costume that gave the men in the audience 'a glimpse of the shape of the female body, displayed by a girl who was visibly embarrassed at exhibiting herself in this way' *(The Invisible Woman*, 1990)? What impact did the infertility caused by gonorrhoea have on Katherine Mansfield?

Tomalin's biographies are painstakingly researched: she revisits primary sources to tease out new facts in a way that makes her books read, in part, like detective stories. She is not afraid to speculate or to use her own experiences as a wife and the mother of five children to guess at how her subjects might have felt. In the following extract from *The Invisible Woman*, she considers how Nelly Ternan, the actress and close companion of Charles Dickens, might have felt if the rumours that she had born Dickens a child and lost the baby had been accurate:

Inconvenient and upsetting for Dickens, but for Nelly it would have been infinitely worse. To give birth, to cherish for a few months perhaps, and then to lose a baby, is a terrible thing. It becomes more terrible if the child is not to be acknowledged and can be remembered only as a dreamlike guilty secret; first shame, then love, then grief. If Nelly went through this ordeal, rawly painful in itself, it must have raised in her mind the question as to whether there would be more babies for her, and what their circumstances were likely to be; whether she would ever be in a position to take pleasure and pride in children of her own. These were questions to which Dickens would scarcely have been able to offer reassuring answers.

▶ In this extract which are the key words that show that Tomalin is speculating about the relationship between Dickens and Nelly?

Tomalin's early books were primarily concerned with women who had slipped off the historical radar. Nelly Ternan is the 'invisible woman'; her biography of Katherine Mansfield is subtitled 'A Secret Life'. *Mrs Jordan's Profession* reclaims the life of one of the most popular actresses of the 18th and early 19th century, who had ten children by the Duke of Clarence, the future King William IV, but whose existence was edited out of Victorian biographies of the monarch. Dora Jordan invented her own name and never married; she earned a great deal of money but died penniless.

Tomalin has said in interviews that she is running out of women to write about and her last two biographies have taken famous male writers as their subjects: *Samuel Pepys: The Unequalled Self* (2002) and *Thomas Hardy: The Time-torn Man* (2006). In writing about well-known literary figures she faced the challenge of finding a new way of interpreting their lives. In the case of Hardy she placed greater emphasis on his poetry than previous biographers.

When writing about the 17th-century diarist, Pepys (1633–1703), she sought a new perspective that added to Pepys' own life writing in his vivid and extremely well-known diaries – which he stopped writing in 1669, thirty-four years before his death. Her solution was to provide a rich historical context that illuminates his writings. With this book, Tomalin won the overall Whitbread Book Award in 2002, beating her husband, the novelist and playwright Michael Frayn, whose *Spies* won the best novel category.

Margaret Forster: experiments in life writing

Although Margaret Forster's first commercial success was the novel *Georgy Girl* (1965), she has tried most forms of life writing. The themes that she explores, such as the changing role of women and family memory, feature in both her fiction and non-fiction. Occasionally one work feeds another. In the historical novel

Lady's Maid (1990), Forster revisits the relationship between Robert and Elizabeth Browning from the viewpoint of her maid, Elizabeth Wilson. Forster originally wrote about Browning in her biography of the poet in 1988, and she includes an afterword to *Lady's Maid* in which she explains how much of the novel is based on fact.

Forster has experimented with the traditional form of life writing in other ways. In 1978 she published *Memoirs Of A Victorian Gentleman, William Makepeace Thackeray*, an 'autobiography' of the poet. Her *Diary of an Ordinary Woman* tells the story of Millicent King, a woman whose life spans the 20th century, and, although the cover states that the book is a novel, many readers assumed it was true. In *Hidden Lives: A Family Memoir* (1995), and its sequel, *Precious Lives*, she explores her own family history to tell the story of three generations of women. Her **authorised** biography of Daphne du Maurier was hampered by a revelation after she had finished writing the book – but before she had delivered the manuscript to the publishers – that du Maurier had had lesbian relationships. She was able to edit her work to take into account this new fact but it remained for later biographers to make a more leisurely assessment of how this might have influenced du Maurier's novels.

Richard Holmes: biography as pursuit

It is common for a biographer to feel a great empathy with their subject, but Richard Holmes has gone further than any other biographer in identifying with the writers whose lives he has investigated. He has pursued their stories and this pursuit has become part of his writings in which he sees parallels in history with his own life. His books and essays are a mixture of biography, autobiography and travel writing.

Holmes finished his first book, *Shelley: The Pursuit* (1974), when he was twenty-nine, the same age at which Shelley drowned in the Gulf of Spezia – as Holmes points out in his preface to the 1994 edition. At the start of the eight-hundred-page life he explains his approach:

> The reader who asks what is literally 'new' partly misunderstands the nature of this kind of biographical research. It is more the case that perspectives change, 'old' facts and events and documents take on new significance and relations, while fresh local research puts events and experiences in a new setting, drawing in elements that before had not been given proper consideration. What is constantly new is not the past itself, but the way we look back on it.

In *Footsteps, Adventures of a Romantic Biographer* (1985) he outlines how he came to choose each of his subjects and the almost mystical ties that link him to each one. In 1964 he slept rough to retrace the journey of the Scottish writer

Robert Louis Stevenson through the Cévennes and describes sitting naked in the Loire river, cleaning his teeth, 'I felt rapturous and slightly mad.' Aware that Stevenson had worn a large silver gypsy ring on his wedding finger – even though he was unmarried – Holmes buys a tin ring from a gypsy stall. As he entered Langogne, the biggest place he had visited in days, 'something strange happened':

> The feeling that Stevenson was actually waiting for me, in person, grew overwhelmingly strong. It was almost like a hallucination. I began to look for him in the crowds, in the faces at the café doors, at hotel windows. I went back to the bridge, took off my hat, rather formally as if to meet a friend, and paced up and down, waiting for some sort of sign. People glanced at me: I felt an oddity, not knowing quite what I was doing, or looking for. The twilight thickened; bats began to dart over the river. I watched their flickering flight over the gleaming surface, from one bank to the other.

Holmes describes his experience as a type of 'haunting'.

> It was important for me, because it was probably the first time that I caught an inkling of what a process (indeed an entire vocation) called 'biography' really means. I had never thought about it before. 'Biography' meant a book about someone's life. Only, for me, it was to become a kind of pursuit, a tracking of the physical trail of someone's path through the past, a following of footsteps. You would never catch them; no, you would never quite catch them. But maybe, if you were lucky, you might write about the pursuit of that fleeting figure in such a way as to bring it alive in the present.

Holmes follows in the footsteps of Wordsworth and Mary Wollstonecraft in Revolutionary Paris as he experiences the Paris riots of the 1960s, and wanders through Italy on the trail of Shelley and his Romantic friends. He describes Shelley's drowning as 'like a death in the family' and worked on his biography virtually non-stop every day for fourteen months. He flushes out suppressions by Victorian biographers and pieces together a new version of the claims that Shelley fathered an illegitimate child in Italy.

Through biographies such as his life of the poet Samuel Taylor Coleridge, which took fifteen years to research, Holmes mixes exhaustive research with a technique of empathising with his subject and blending in historical context.

Ethics and biography

While Victorian biographers were coy about several aspects of their subjects' lives, there are few topics that a modern biographer will shy away from. The threat of legal action and the biographer's reputation – often more than their subject's – are usually the only factors that might make them hesitate before tackling a particularly personal or lurid topic. Indeed, some biographers feel under pressure from their publisher to produce a sensational angle or new item of information, a focus that Sigmund Freud – and later – the novelist Joyce Carol Oates described as 'pathography'.

The modern biographer is unlikely to feel inhibited about examining their subject's sexuality and sex life, their addictions and the intimate details of their health. Many would argue that such topics are vital to a proper understanding of their subject's literary output. Does the misogyny that some critics have detected in T.S. Eliot's poems mean that he was gay or is it more likely to reflect his inability to deal with female sexuality? What relevance does Daphne du Maurier's lesbianism, her 'Venetian' tendencies as the family referred to them, have to her novels? Was Bruce Chatwin's closet homosexuality linked in any way to his style of melding autobiography, fiction and fact in his writing? (Nicholas Shakespeare certainly thought his double life was relevant and in his authorised biography examined Chatwin's homosexual affairs in detail.)

Several highly respected biographies of recent times have examined whether their subjects were suffering from sexually transmitted diseases, for example, Claire Tomalin in her life of Katherine Mansfield and Kathryn Hughes in her biography of Mrs Beeton, the influential cookery writer and author of *The Book of Household Management*. An article in the *The Times Literary Supplement*, which put forward a theory that Thomas Hardy had given his wife Emma syphilis and that this explained her mental instability, led to a heated and protracted exchanges of letters. Correspondents argued about the likelihood of this and whether Hardy's poems provided any clues. Tomalin asserted her belief that: 'The fact that there were other members of her family who showed signs of mental instability rather suggests that her eccentricities were part of a family pattern, and Hardy's poem "The Interloper" may be read in this context.' For the full debate see: www.timesonline.co.uk/tol/global/article2342966.ece

▶ Ackroyd's biography of Dickens includes the line, 'Every biography is a prisoner of its time.' In what way do you think the inclusion of intimate details and attempts to diagnose health problems in late 20th- and 21st-century literary biographies bears this out?

Anne Sexton and the debate over privacy

When Diane Wood Middlebrook (1939–2007), a professor of English at Stanford University, published her biography of the American poet, Anne Sexton (1928–1974) in 1991 it caused an uproar. Like her friend, Sylvia Plath, Sexton's poetry was highly autobiographical and drew on her long periods of mental ill health and addiction. But it was not these topics that made the biography so controversial.

Sexton met Sylvia Plath at Boston University where they became close friends and influenced each other's work. Sexton published her first collection of poems, *To Bedlam and Part Way Back*, in 1960. As in later collections, her poems focused on her inner turmoil and her time spent visiting a psychotherapist. She won a Pulitzer Prize in 1967 for *Live or Die* (1966) but committed suicide in 1974 at the age of forty-five.

Middlebrook's biography contains intimate details of Sexton's life, including her alcoholism, mental illness, sexual abuse of her daughter and her many affairs, including one with a therapist (who is not named in the book). But the aspect of the book that provoked controversy was that Sexton's psychiatrist, Dr Martin T. Orne, who treated her from 1956 to 1964 and who encouraged her to write, taped his sessions with Sexton and allowed Middlebrook to listen to 300 audiotapes – a task that took her two years, although she said they contained no revelations but merely confirmed what she already knew. The biographer also found a folder of Sexton's earlier poems marked 'Not to be seen by anybody' and decided not to publish them.

Criticism for using the tapes fell mainly on Orne, who wrote a foreword to the biography, and came primarily from his colleagues who argued that the privacy of the therapy room was sacrosanct. Dr Willard Gaylin, a Columbia University psychiatry professor and an expert on medical ethics, told *The New York Times* (15 July 1991): 'Doctors have no obligation to history and certainly should not act as a research assistant to a biographer.'

Orne said he recorded the sessions because Sexton suffered from memory loss and listening to the recordings of previous sessions helped her. Both he and her daughter, Dr Linda Gray Sexton, the executor of her mother's literary estate, maintained that Sexton would have approved of releasing the records. Few of Sexton's friends disagreed with the biographer's decision to use the transcripts.

▶ At the time of the controversy, J.D. McClatchy, a poet and critic who edited *Anne Sexton, the Artist and Her Critics*, posed the question: 'Imagine if we suddenly found tapes of the psychiatric sessions of Virginia Woolf. Who would not want to listen?' (*The New York Times*, 15 July 1991). If such tapes were discovered, would it be ethical for a biographer to use them? Does the time that has elapsed after the tapes make any difference to the decision?

Iris Murdoch and the different claims on her life

When Iris Murdoch (1919–1999), the novelist and philosopher, died, readers had several versions of her life to choose from. John Bayley, the critic and academic whom she married in 1956, wrote a memoir, *Iris* (1998), that provided a portrait of their relationship and Murdoch's struggle with Alzheimer's. He followed this with *Iris and the Friends* and *Widower's House*. His versions offer a reverential view of his wife. 'Her humility ... seems itself so unpretentious, unlike most humility' (*Iris*) is typical of his approach, although he shows an unflinching view of the illness she suffered from. Occasionally, Bayley provides an insight into her novels by pointing out the origins of an idea – how, for example, a piece of pottery discovered on a swim in France provides the spark that becomes *The Bell*, and how the green Riley car that appears in *The Sandcastle* has its roots in a car that Bailey found for her.

At seven hundred pages and nearly two thousand footnotes, Peter Conradi's authorised biography, *Iris Murdoch: A Life* (2001), offers a more academic and dispassionate approach, although it was written by a close friend of the couple's. A film of her life, *Iris* starring Judi Dench and Kate Winslet as the old and young Murdoch, appeared in the same year and placed the emphasis on her as a victim of Alzheimer's.

The novelist, columnist and historian A.N. Wilson set out to offer what he saw as a more rounded version, 'an anti-biography' which would restore the reputation of a great writer who had become stereotyped as 'Alzheimer's Lady'. Wilson was Bayley's pupil at Oxford and had been the couple's friend for thirty years, but in *Iris Murdoch as I Knew Her* (2003) he describes her drinking, promiscuity and deception. Bayley is portrayed as a bumbling fool and the book is full of stories of the couple's meanness and the squalor in which they lived. Wilson believed: 'The best picture of Iris Murdoch is actually to be found in the novels of Iris Murdoch.'

Of all the versions Wilson's received the worst reviews, but one critic provided some helpful advice:

> What to do? Don't read Wilson's book unless you've read Bayley or Conradi or both. Do if you have. You'll get things right if it is Bayley and Conradi who remain with you, retuned by Wilson's twist. Applied in this way, *Iris Murdoch As I Knew Her* is a useful work.
>
> (Galen Strawson, *Guardian*, 6 September 2003)

▶ Is it possible for a biographer to write an objective life about someone they do not like? What clues might help the reader to know whether the biographer is being fair to his or her subject?

Autobiography and authorised biography

While recent memoirs appear to be unflinchingly honest, writers who choose to produce their own life history are not always the most accurate or thorough biographers. Just as biographers bring their own prejudices to their subject, an author may not always be the best judge of their work and the biographical influences on it.

An authorised biography is one in which the subject or his or her family give their blessing to the book. The amount of co-operation can vary from allowing the biographer to quote from certain letters, diaries and works held in copyright to giving them unrestricted access to all archives. Often the subject or their estate will request to see the manuscript before it is printed and may demand that changes are made. In some cases the subject or their estate chooses the biographer. Thus George Bernard Shaw's estate commissioned a new biography in the 1960s and asked the Society of Authors, which acted as its agents, to approach Michael Holroyd. The arrangement allowed the estate to withdraw their authorisation if they felt the book was badly written, but they could not stop its publication as an unauthorised life – instead, they would charge fees for quotations that would otherwise have been free.

Holroyd summed up the uneasy relationship between the biographer and the descendents of his or her subject in *Works on Paper* (2002):

> Biographers rely on the families of their subjects in much the same way as portrait painters rely on their sitters. Both are grateful for essential help, but they cannot let this gratitude interfere with what they see.

An author or their family can be equally *unhelpful* if they are not keen on the idea of a biographer. T.S. Eliot announced that he did not want a biography and when Peter Ackroyd started work on his life, Eliot's estate refused to allow him to quote from Eliot's published work, except for 'fair comment in a critical context', that is the usual minimum legal limit without breaching copyright law. Ackroyd was banned from quoting *anything* from the unpublished work and correspondence. Although this would cause dismay in most biographers, some critics found that a more sparing use of quotes made for a better biography. Where he could not quote he paraphrased. He consulted other archives and used the diaries of Eliot's first wife and comments from surviving friends.

Travel writer Paul Theroux found himself in a similar position when writing a memoir of the Nobel prize-winning novelist and his one-time friend, V.S. Naipaul. Theroux met Naipaul in Uganda where he was teaching and Naipaul, already a famous author, was writer-in-residence. Their friendship, however, disintegrated once they returned to Britain. When Theroux decided to write about their relationship, Naipaul only allowed him to quote briefly from the letters Naipaul had written to him and refused to let him see the letters Theroux had written over a period of thirty years. Theroux was, in effect, denied access to his own letters. Lawyers urged changes and deletions and warned that Naipaul was wealthy enough to sue him. In 1998 Theroux published *Sir Vidia's Shadow* in which he described Naipaul as a snob and a racist. Most reviews criticised Theroux for his audacity and accused him of jealousy.

A decade later Patrick French published an authorised biography of Naipaul, *The World Is What It Is*. French had full access to his subject, who was now in his late seventies, and his archives; the book makes many of the claims that Theroux had first stated and others that he had been too afraid to. It describes in great detail Naipaul's affairs, his treatment of his dying wife and the speed with which she was replaced after her death. Naipaul, it seems, did not demand any changes to the manuscript.

▶ Can you think of an author whose work you admire but whose views you disagree with? How important is to bear in mind the historical and cultural contexts in which a person was writing when assessing their attitudes to subjects such as race and gender? Why might an author and their family change their views on an authorised biography as they grow older?

Assignments

1   Jane Austen wrote under the title 'A Lady', Mary Ann Evans became George Eliot and the Brontë sisters took the pseudonyms Currer, Ellis and Acton Bell. Examine the reasons why women writers chose to hide their identity and how pseudonyms affected the reception of their work. Compare the motives behind the anonymous publication of *Primary Colors* in 1996 and *Gulliver's Travels* in 1726 and the ways in which anonymity boosted sales of both.

2   Consider Samuel Johnson's views on the value to a biographer of 'a short conversation' with a servant (see page 17, above). What are the dangers of using the views of 'servants', or other minor players, in a biography? Compare the use of the testimonies of servants in Mrs Gaskell's *Life of Charlotte Brontë* and Alison Light's *Mrs Woolf and the Servants* (see page 21, above, and the extract in Part 3, page 92).

3   Discover what you can about the political climate in Britain in 1599. How does this knowledge affect your assessment of the type of plays and the key characters Shakespeare was working on at this time, as well as his choice of Plutarch as a source and inspiration?

4   Virginia Woolf, Anne Sexton, Sylvia Plath and Janet Frame each suffered from mental illness. Examine how this represents itself in their work and compare it to the way in which biographers have related their instability to their work.

2 | Approaching the texts

- What factors affect a biographer's approach to their subject?

- What similarities and contrasts may be shown by the range of writers under consideration?

- What kinds of life writing do novelists and poets write?

The growth of literary biography

The Whitbread Literary Awards (now the Costa Book Awards) were launched in 1971 and from the start included a category for biography. Michael Meyer was the first winner of the biography section for his life of the playwright Henrik Ibsen. Since then, biographies of writers have made up around half the winners, while books about the lives of politicians, artists, painters, composers and other historical figures have accounted for the remaining half. Richard Holmes' *Coleridge: Early Visions* and Claire Tomalin's *Samuel Pepys: The Unequalled Self* took the top prize of Whitbread Book of the Year in 1989 and 2002 respectively.

Figures produced by Nielsen BookScan show that the number of new biographies published in the UK peaked in 2003 at 2,328 and for autobiography a year later at 2,070. In 2007, the most recent year for which figures were available, 488 new biographies were published and 271 new autobiographies. Within these figures literary biographies jostle for attention with books about the lives of footballers, politicians, pop singers and models. But, despite the sharp decline in the number of new titles, biographies are still capable of selling in large quantities: 1.9 million biographies and 2.5 million autobiographies in 2007. This demand has meant that the most popular biographers can command the sorts of advances on sales of their books that would be impressive in any genre.

▶ Look at the extract from *The Silent Woman: Sylvia Plath and Ted Hughes* by Janet Malcolm (Part 3, page 93). To what extent do you agree that the relationship between biographer and reader sees them 'tiptoeing down the corridor together, to stand in front of the bedroom door and try to peep through the keyhole'?

Choosing a biographical subject

Biographer and subject will 'live' together for several years. Norman Sherry, for example, spent over a quarter of a century working on his three-volume biography of Graham Greene. It is important, then, that the biographer can sustain their passion for the subject for the time that it takes to write the book.

Researching a life involves considerable expense and most biographers are reluctant to commit themselves to a subject until they have secured a publisher's contract. Even then, the advance may not cover the cost of research, which is likely to include travel as well as fees to quote from the subject's published work. Several factors can influence a publisher's decision to commission a biography or a biographer to seek a publisher. One reason might be the availability of new material. This might be official documents which have been released after a certain number of years; or it might be the planned publication of diaries and letters by a literary estate – for example, Leonard Woolf's publication of his wife's writings over several years. It might be the unexpected discovery of new facts and sources, although very often the biographer uncovers these as part of their research – such as Mark Bostridge's revelation about the circumstances surrounding the death of Vera Brittain's brother (see page 28, above).

Anniversaries – either of an author's death, birth or a significant landmark in their life, such as the publication of their greatest work – can provide the impetus for a biography. Some two thousand letters written by the poet Philip Larkin were deposited at Hull University (where he was Librarian) by his niece in 2008, and are expected to be published in 2010 to mark the twenty-fifth anniversary of his death.

The point at which an author's work goes out of copyright can play a part in the timing of a biography because it makes it easier – and cheaper – to quote from their writing. Until 1 January 1996 copyright in the UK lasted for fifty years from the end of the year of the author's death, but has since been extended to seventy years. There are some exceptions to this rule, such as non-European authors and material that was unpublished at the time of the author's death.

Sometimes it is sheer coincidence that more than one biography of the same writer appears at the same time. This is what happened when Ian Thomson and Carole Angier raced to publish their biographies of Primo Levi in 2002, and in September 1997 when Claire Tomalin and David Nokes both produced lives of Jane Austen.

Practical considerations

The huge amount of research involved means that most biographers prefer to stay within one historical period, so that each book they write builds on previous knowledge and allows them to identify trends and connections. Claire Tomalin's subjects have, on the whole, not included writers who were born after Queen Victoria's reign. Peter Ackroyd, on the other hand, has ranged from Chaucer to T.S. Eliot, but he is an exceptionally prolific writer for whom London, rather than one historical period, provides a constant, over-arching theme.

The biographer must possess the necessary skills or be prepared to acquire them. It would be impossible to write a good literary biographer of Leo Tolstoy without the ability to read his novels, and other sources, in the original Russian. It would be equally difficult to write about Shakespeare without a thorough knowledge of Elizabethan and Jacobean England. Proximity to primary sources is also important. If the biographer is in America and the main sources are in Britain, he or she will have to consider whether they can fund the research trips to study them.

The amount and accessibility of sources are vital considerations, but problems with both will fail to deter the dogged biographer. Shakespeare scholars have had scant facts to grapple with, but this has not stopped several books appearing in recent years which offer a new perspective on his life. Charles Nicholl's *The Lodger: Shakespeare on Silver Street* (2007) focuses on a court case as a way of teasing out the story of Shakespeare's later life and how this might have influenced his plays. In October 1604 Shakespeare was an upstairs lodger in a house in Silver Street, north of Cheapside in London, when his landlord's daughter, Marie Mountjoy, asked him to encourage her suitor, Stephen Belott (who was her father's apprentice), towards marriage after initial plans had stalled, mainly over her father's reluctance to provide a dowry. Shakespeare stepped in by assuring them that the dowry would appear and by uniting them in a 'handfast' – at the time a legally binding form of uniting a couple and typically followed by a church wedding. (Rosalind and Orlando perform something similar in *As You Like It*.) When, in 1612, Belott took his father-in-law to court over his reluctance to produce a dowry, Shakespeare appeared as a witness.

Nicholl's book is based on documents that scholars had been aware of since the beginning of the 20th century. Dr Charles William Wallace, associate professor of English at the University of Nebraska, and his wife, Hulda, unearthed the evidence in 1909 when they were searching through the Court of Request papers in the Public Record Office (now the National Archives) at Kew, in South London. Although the documents, which contain Shakespeare's signatures, were widely known of, it took Nicholl to place them firmly in the context of Shakespeare's life. As Nicholl points out, the Belott *v.* Mountjoy case provides a vital piece of primary information – an address for Shakespeare in London – and Nicholl concludes that he was probably living in Silver Street when he wrote *Othello*, *Measure for Measure*, *All's Well That Ends Well*, *Timon of Athens* and the beginnings of *King Lear*.

Nicholl uses a mass of other sources – archaeological remains, maps, parish registers, subsidy rolls, casebooks, woodcuts, wills and inventories – to recreate that part of London. He shows the reader how Shakespeare would have experienced life in the capital and how that experience relates to Shakespeare's plays. His approach allows the reader to join in the search for the shadowy lodger, who gradually takes shape as the book progresses. In his review of the book, fellow Shakespeare biographer James Shapiro called *The Lodger* 'Part biography, part detective story'.

In the following extract Nicholl describes in detail the document on which his book is based and in doing so places the reader by his side as he views it:

Shakespeare's deposition was exhibited for a while in the Record Office Museum, mounted under glass, but is now back where it ought to be, safely and unceremoniously stored in a stout cardboard box at the National Archives's new headquarters in Kew. There, duly vetted, one may consult it. Ensconced behind two locked doors in the 'Safe Room', I carefully extract from the box this sheet of greyish, coarse-grained paper which Shakespeare once handled, rather less carefully, on a Monday morning nearly four centuries ago. It is hard to say quite what the page has which the photographic reproductions of it do not. The signature is clearer, of course. That dot inside the arcade of the W is very sharp: it stares out like a beady eye. The ill-formed K is perceivable as a sudden blotching of ink – a malfunction of the unfamiliar courtroom pen, perhaps. Beyond this one has to resort to vaguer sensations. This bit of paper has presence, or anyway pedigree – an unbroken lineage back to Shakespeare's writing hand.

▶ How does the style of this extract compare with the extract from *1599* (Part 3, page 98) in which Shapiro analyses another document? How is each biographer using different documents to engage with the reader? What do you think might be the benefits of consulting an original document – for example, a letter, diary entry or early draft of a manuscript? How do you think the move away from handwritten documents and towards electronic communication will affect the work of future literary biographers?

Empathy with the subject

It is usual, and often helpful, for the biographer to feel a connection with the author whose life they are dissecting. Margaret Forster has said that she did not choose Daphne du Maurier, but that du Maurier chose her. The process started when Forster was reaching up to retrieve a book from a high shelf and *Rebecca*, which she had not read since she was thirteen, toppled down. Forster was looking for a new biographical subject – and when she reread the opening sequence of *Rebecca*, it prompted her to find out more about the author. A few days later du Maurier died and Forster was asked to write her obituary for the *Sunday Times*. Fate, or a series of coincidences, had led Forster to her subject.

Hermione Lee ends her biography of Virginia Woolf with a postscript entitled 'Biographer'. It is a rare interlude in which she writes in the first person to reveal something of the connection between herself and her subject, as well as describing how Woolf has appeared in different forms to different biographers. The section begins:

I was born in February 1948, three years after the end of the war and seven years after Virginia Woolf's death. I grew up in a literary household which had all her books: I can't remember not having heard of her. When I was eight or nine I went away on a visit (this was rather unusual for me) and stayed the night with friends. There was one book on the table by my bed. It was the 1951 orange Penguin edition of *The Waves*, with, on the cover the price, 1s.6d., the words 'Fiction' in orange letters along the sides, and, on either side of the image of a penguin, the words 'Complete' and 'Unabridged'. On the back was a brief biography of Virginia Woolf underneath the 1929 Lenare photograph. I don't think I was aware of any of these details, but I do vividly remember starting to read the first few pages, without understanding much of what was going on, and feeling as if I had happened on a secret language which belonged to me. It was part of the excitement of being away from home on my own. This was my discovery. I didn't get very far, and I don't remember my subsequent return to the novel. But that sense of a secret discovery remained with me, and left an echo-track in later readings.

Alison Light was equally honest with her readers when she revealed the motivation behind her book, *Mrs Woolf and the Servants, The Hidden Heart of Domestic Service* (2007), in which she explores Woolf's complex feelings towards her servants and the lower classes in general. In the preface to the book Light explains:

I have my own personal reasons for wanting to write this book. My grandmother, my mother's mother, Lilian Heffren, was a live-in servant for a time and her memories, which I grew up with, were always at the back of my mind. Like Nellie Boxall [one of Woolf's servants], she was born in the last decade of the nineteenth century. She too went into service as a young girl barely in her teens straight from the orphanage (the local workhouse), where she'd been placed after her parents' death. Her memories were grim and she often talked of being 'treated like dirt' by other women.

Light goes on to explain how her own circumstances changed while she was researching the book and that her experiences altered many of her views. She nursed her husband while he struggled with cancer, and believes that she approached the book differently when she returned to work on it after his death:

It made me think and feel differently about the place of mourning in Virginia Woolf's life and it seemed important to write about how that affected her in becoming a writer. It also made the question of her dependence on others look and feel different: this suddenly had an inevitability about it, which I had seen face to face. Dependence was no longer a question of whether, so much as when. And I also came to think that the capacity to entrust one's life to the care of others, including strangers, and for this to happen safely and in comfort, without abuse, is crucial to any decent community and to any society worth the name.

Many female biographers, whether literary or not, write predominately about women or the key part played by a woman in a writer's life. This has been the case with Forster, Lee and – until her later biographies – Tomalin, and may partly be because the writer feels a special empathy with the struggle provoked by their gender. The problem, though, for biographers is that there is a limited supply of well-known female writers worthy of a literary biography.

For other biographers their subject's sexuality sparks empathy. Diana Souhami has said that when she first started writing she made a conscious decision to write about lesbians. Her books include *The Trials of Radclyffe Hall*, about the author of one of the very first lesbian novels, *The Well of Loneliness*, and *Gertrude and Alice: Gertrude Stein and Alice B. Toklas*, about the American writer and her companion, Alice B. Toklas. In *Mrs Keppel and Her Daughter*, she tells the story of Violet Trefusis, the daughter of Edward VII's mistress, and her scandalous love affair with Vita Sackville-West. But Souhami's work is not restricted to gay women. In one of her most recent books, *Selkirk's Island* she takes as her subject Alexander Selkirk, whose adventures inspired Daniel Defoe to write *Robinson Crusoe*.

Sexuality is just one aspect of a famous writer's life that might draw a biographer to their subject. Ethnicity, politics and religion are others. When Richard Holmes was a young man living in an attic room in London in the 1960s and observing the student riots in Paris, he identified – he said later, 'naively' – with the French Revolution as seen by the English Romantics.

> The whole ethos of the Sixties – that youthful explosion of idealism, colour, music, sex, hallucinogenic states, hyperbolic language and easy money ... was based on a profoundly romantic rejection of conventional society, the old order, the establishment, the classical, the square (and also, in fact, austerity).
> > Bliss was it in that dawn to be alive,
> > But to be young was very heaven!
> > [William Wordsworth, *The Prelude 1805*] (from *Footsteps*)

Norman Sherry has said that when he first met Graham Greene, the novelist appeared to be dismayed to discover that Sherry was Catholic but to have brightened up when Sherry qualified this piece of information by saying that he was a lapsed Catholic. This must surely have given him a special insight into the religious crises – and in particular loss of faith – that feature in so many of Greene's novels, such as *Brighton Rock*, in which the young thug, Pinkie, is a lapsed Catholic who appears to find it easy to kill but who fears damnation.

▶ Look at the books written by a particular biographer – you can usually find a list at the beginning of one of their books or on their website. Can you see any connections between the subjects they have written about? Are there any 'odd ones out'?

Structuring a life

Traditionally, biographies and autobiographies have followed a straight, linear narrative, starting with the subject's birth and proceeding with a chronological account of their life until their death and concluding, perhaps, with an assessment of their work – a sort of literary afterlife. It is surprising how many biographies, even ones that are original in many other ways, start with a description of weather – often on the day the subject was born: 'The winter of 1775 was a hard one' (*Jane Austen, A Life* by Claire Tomalin); 'Sheet-lightning split the sky over London on the evening of 12 May 1907 and thunder rumbled long into the night' (*Daphne du Maurier*, Margaret Forster).

This 'cradle-to-grave' approach has the advantage of clarity. The reader is unlikely to become confused but, at the same time, the narrative can have a plodding inevitability to it. An unbending, chronological structure is particularly challenging if the subject had a very long life or one in which their literary output – or other dramatic peaks – are concentrated in one section of their life. Writing a biography of Stella Gibbons (1902–1990), for example, would be challenging. Gibbons lived to be eighty-eight but wrote her most successful novel, *Cold Comfort Farm*, a witty parody of rural fiction at the beginning of the 20th century, in 1932. Harper Lee would make an even trickier subject. She was born in 1926 and wrote *To Kill A Mockingbird* in 1960, for which she won the Pulitzer Prize, but it has been her only book to date and she has spent the last forty years hiding from the public gaze.

Biographers have to decide how much of their subject's family history they will include and at what point they will introduce this 'backstory'. In *Lives* Plutarch believes it is important to discuss a great man's forebears. He begins his portrait of Antony with a description of his antecedents:

> Antony's grandfather was the orator Antonius, who, as a member of Sulla's faction, was killed by Marius, and his father was Antonius surnamed Creticus, who was not particularly well known or distinguished in the public domain, but was a fair and honourable man, and above all a generous one …

In the late 20th century biographers have usually preferred to start their biographies by setting the historical scene and introducing some of the characters who will feature in the story of the life that is about to be told. The first chapter in Claire Tomalin's biography of Jane Austen is headed '1775' and begins:

> The winter of 1775 was a hard one. On 11 November the naturalist Gilbert White saw that the trees around his Hampshire village of Selborne had lost almost all their leaves. 'Trees begin to be naked,' he wrote in his diary. Fifteen miles away, higher up in the Downs, in

the village of Steventon, the rector's wife was expecting the birth of her seventh child from day to day as the last leaves fell. She was thirty-six and had been married for eleven years. Four sturdy little boys ran about the parsonage and the big garden at the back, with its yard and outhouses, rising to the fields and woodland beyond. The eldest, James, at ten already showed promise as a scholar, sharing his father's taste in books, and the only daughter, Cassy, kept her mother entertained with her constant chatter as she followed her round the house and out to visit the dairy and the chickens and ducks. Cassy would be three in January. Outside Mr Austen's study the house was seldom entirely quiet.

The November days went by and the rains set in, keeping the boys indoors; by the end of the month it was dark in the house at three in the afternoon, and dinner had to be eaten very promptly if they were to do without candles. Still no baby had appeared. December came, bringing an epidemic of colds and feverish complaints. There was a sharp frost, putting ice on the ponds, enough for the boys to go sliding; then, on the 16th, White noted, 'Fog, sun, sweet day.' The 16th of December was the day of Jane Austen's birth ...

▶ How many people has Tomalin introduced in the opening of her biography? What sort of picture does she paint of the Austen household?

Peter Ackroyd, by comparison, starts his biography of Dickens with a prologue headed with three quotations: Thomas Carlyle on Dickens, a line from Vladimir Nabokov's *The Real Life of Sebastian Knight* and from Fyodor Dostoevksy's *The Brothers Karamazov*. His narrative begins:

Charles Dickens was dead. He lay on a narrow green sofa – but there was room enough for him, so spare had he become – in the dining room of Gad's Hill Place. He had died in the house which he had first seen as a small boy and which his father had pointed out to him as a suitable object of his ambitions; so great was his father's hold on his life that, forty years later, he had bought it ...

After a six-page prologue Ackroyd returns to a conventional chronology in Chapter one:

Charles Dickens was born on the seventh of February 1812, the year of victory and the year of hardship. He came crying into the world in a small first-floor bedroom in an area known as New Town or Mile End, just on the outskirts of Portsmouth where his father, John Dickens, worked in the Naval Pay Office.

But Ackroyd's note to Chapter one is as enlightening as the main text:

> No one has written more poignantly about Charles Dickens's
> childhood than Charles Dickens, although his aptitude for fiction
> was such that not all his reminiscences are free of invention. One of
> the hardest tasks for any biographer, in fact, lies in the attempt to
> separate the real truths from the penumbra of romance, nostalgia
> and fantasy which surrounds them. For, in a sense, Dickens's
> childhood can be found everywhere – in the elaborate narratives of
> *Great Expectations* and *David Copperfield* no less than in shorter
> journalistic essays ... But there are levels of truth, just as there are
> different levels of narrative. The fictional accounts can be taken
> just as that – fiction, even though there are many passages in the
> novels which reflect aspects of Dickens's childhood aspirations.
> Then there are the essays which he wrote as himself or as the
> 'Uncommercial Traveller'; in these there tends to be a charming if
> sometimes confusing mixture of fictional narrative and true memory.
> And then there is the famous 'autobiographical fragment' which
> Dickens employed in *David Copperfield*, and which John Forster later
> published in the life of his friend. This again owes as much to the
> tradition of autobiographical writing as it does to Dickens's memories
> of his childhood, but there is no doubt that in the general drift of the
> narrative is to be found an essential truth about Dickens's childhood.
> Dickens also sometimes spoke to Forster about his earlier years and
> these oral reminiscences, to be found in the early pages of Forster's
> biography, have the ring of genuine and momentary recollection.
> These, at least, we can transmit without the precaution of exegesis.

▶ In what ways does a note such as the above change the way a reader would
approach the text? What difficulties would Ackroyd face if he had decided to include
this note in the main body of the book?

Footnotes and literary asides

Footnotes serve several purposes. Their main use is to show the reader the sources
from which the biographer has gathered their information. These might range
from newspaper cuttings to a coroner's report, unpublished letters, interviews with
the author or a television documentary. Footnotes help the reader to follow the
biographer's trail and to assess whether they have been true to the clues they have
found or whether they have jumped to conclusions not justified by the evidence.

Most academic books and serious literary biographies have footnotes. It has
become the practice in books aimed at the general public to print footnotes at the
end of the book, rather than the foot of the page where they can be distracting.
Some biographies use 'endnotes', rather than footnotes; they include less detail but
give an overview of the main sources for each chapter.

Biographers also use footnotes to shift extraneous material that may nevertheless be interesting from the main text to a place where it will not interrupt the **narrative** drive or **mood** of the book. Towards the end of her biography of Virginia Woolf, Hermione Lee describes in poignant detail Woolf's suicide, the inquest and the cremation that Leonard went to alone, ending this paragraph with the sentences:

> The ashes, which, also to his surprise, had been presented to him in a pretentiously elaborate casket, he buried under one of the great elms in the garden which they had called 'Leonard' and 'Virginia'. He had a tablet made with a quotation from *The Waves* ('Against you I will fling myself unvanquished and unyielding, O Death!') to place over the ashes.

The footnote relating to these sentences provides the sources for Lee's description, together with some additional detail: 'One of the elms blew down in 1943, the other died years later. The ashes and the tablet were moved to the centre of the garden, under the Tomlin bust of VW.'

▶ Do you think Lee was right to move this information to a footnote? If she had incorporated this detail into the chapter how would it have altered the **tone** of the writing?

In addition to footnotes, other biographers have paused to insert literary asides in which they expand on themes that might be difficult to weave into the main narrative or to offer a contrast to the main narrative – as in the case of Ackroyd's *Dickens*, when the biographer meets his subject. Kathryn Hughes' biography of Mrs Beeton includes several 'interludes' in which she provides historical context or expands on themes from Mrs Beeton's main literary work, the *Book of Household Management*. In one interlude Hughes explains that the *Book of Household Management* is vague on the timing of every meal except for dinner, but this was because the 'gastronomic shape of the day' was changing. In another Hughes ponders how Beeton's 'Useful Soup for Benevolent Purposes' related to the Victorian attitude to feeding the poor.

Assessing the truth in autobiography and memoir

Footnotes do not generally appear in autobiography and memoir. The reader – at least before the reviews appear – has to rely on the author's honesty and self-awareness.

Muriel Spark (1918–2006), herself a biographer, as well as a poet and short story writer (but best known for her novel *The Prime of Miss Jean Brodie*, 1961, about an Edinburgh schoolmistress and her favoured pupils), sets out her guiding principles in the introduction to her autobiography, *Curriculum Vitae* (1992):

> I determined to write nothing that cannot be supported by documentary evidence or by eyewitness; I have not relied on my

memory alone, vivid though it is. The disturbing thing about false and erroneous statements is that well-meaning scholars tend to repeat each other. Lies are like fleas hopping from here to there, sucking the blood of the intellect. In my case, the truth is often less flattering, less romantic, but often more interesting than the false story. Truth by itself is neutral and has its own dear beauty; especially in a work of non-fiction it is to be cherished. Besides, false data lead to false premises and those to false conclusions. Is it fair to scholars and students of literature to let them be misled even on the most insignificant matters?

Throughout the book Spark repeatedly quotes incidents that provided inspiration for her literary work: her friend Nita was shot dead by her husband, a tragedy which provided the factual origin for the short story 'Bang-Bang You're Dead'; a teacher smashed a saucer to the ground to quieten a class and this appeared in *The Prime of Miss Jean Brodie*; another teacher, Miss Christina Kay, called her favoured pupils 'crème de la crème', just as Jean Brodie does.

Curriculum Vitae deals with the first thirty-nine years of Spark's life, up to 1957. By the time of her death in 2006 she had moved to Rome, where she lived with her companion, Penelope Jardine, conducted a public feud with her son and lived as a Catholic for half a century. Obituaries and tributes presented another side of Spark's life and took the opportunity to reassess her autobiography, as in this extract from *The Times*.

> But she detested intrusion into her private life, and the book tells very little about Spark herself. She could be prickly and had a reputation for falling out with friends and associates. A former editor, for example, with whom she once shared the ownership of a racehorse, fell from grace when he described her in an interview as 'really quite batty'.
>
> (*The Times*, 17 April 2006)

▶ A writer's autobiography and obituaries written about them offer two views of a life. What are the advantages and perils of both to a literary biographer assessing their subject?

New approaches to biography

1599: Shakespeare – a moment in time

Some biographers have successfully tackled the problem of an uneven dramatic narrative by narrowing their focus to a very precise moment in their subject's life. James Shapiro has done this with great success in *1599: A Year in the Life of William Shakespeare* by choosing a period that was highly significant for Shakespeare as a playwright, and also for the country as a whole. It was the year in which he completed *Henry the Fifth*, wrote *Julius Caesar* and *As You Like It* and drafted *Hamlet*. But it was also a year of rumour and uncertainty for ordinary Elizabethans. The ageing Elizabeth I faced unrest in Ireland, infighting at court and the threat of invasion by Catholic Spain. Shakespeare was dependent on his queen's patronage and knew he had to be sensitive to national events.

In *1599* Shapiro shows how Shakespeare may have been influenced by the political climate of his time. He argues, for example, that a Lenten sermon given at the royal palace at Richmond by one of England's most famous preachers, Lancelot Andrewes, played an important part in the composition of *Henry the Fifth*. (See extract in Part 3, page 98.)

Shapiro's approach is particularly unusual because Shakespeare is often seen as a timeless genius who cannot be pinned down to one historical period. Shapiro points out that Shakespeare's first editors ignored the order in which his plays were written and decided to 'shoehorn' them into categories of comedies, histories and tragedies. As Shapiro says in his preface:

> The commonplace that dramatists are best understood in relation to their time would go unquestioned if the writer in question were Euripides, Ibsen or Beckett. But only recently has the tide begun to turn against a view of Shakespeare as a poet who transcends his age, who wrote, as Samuel Coleridge put it, 'exactly as if of another planet'.

He describes the particular difficulties in writing about Shakespeare's life:

> The time-honoured way biographers have gone about answering this question is to locate the wellspring of Shakespeare's genius in his formative experiences. This is risky enough when writing the lives of modern authors like Virginia Woolf or Sylvia Plath, whose biographers have piles of correspondence, diaries and photographs to sift through. It's nearly impossible with Shakespeare, who left behind neither letters nor diaries. And the only two authentic portraits of Shakespeare to survive are posthumous. ... Biographers can only guess how Shakespeare felt about his mother, father, brothers, sisters, neighbours, friends, schoolmates or employers, or, for that matter, how and even where he spent his adolescence or the crucial 'lost years' between his departure from Stratford and his arrival in London. Those committed to discovering the adult Shakespeare's personality in his formative experiences end up hunting for hints in the plays which they then read back into what little can be surmised about his early years (and since the plays contain almost every kind of relationship and experience imaginable, this is not as hard to do as it sounds) ... Circularity and arbitrariness are only part of the problem: cradle-to-grave biographers of Shakespeare tend to assume that what makes people who they are now made people who they were then.

▶ Shapiro points out that in Shakespeare's England the idea of marrying for love was fairly new. How could awareness of this cultural difference affect a reading of Shakespeare's plays and poetry?

Although the book is called *1599*, Shapiro allows himself to wander from his self-imposed boundaries and he often extrapolates on how the events of that year affected Shakespeare's future work. Shapiro's prologue helps to put 1599 in historical context and the book is then divided into four sections, each headed by the name of a season. By starting with December 1598 Shapiro is able to include a description of the Chamberlain's Men, the group of actors for whom Shakespeare wrote and sometimes performed, and their appearance in front of the Queen. By speculating that they might have chosen *The Second Part of Henry the Fourth*, Shapiro has the chance to expand on the influence of the clownish actor, Will Kemp. Kemp played Sir John Falstaff and many other comic roles until he parted company with Shakespeare – a rift that Shapiro sees as symptomatic of Shakespeare's move towards 'more naturalistic drama'.

Throughout *1599* Shapiro combines a close reading of Shakespeare's plays and poetry with an examination of the political background of the day. A play about *Julius Caesar*, a ruler stabbed to death after intense plotting by the men around him, would seem an unwise choice at a time when Elizabeth I had suffered several attempts on her life, but Shapiro shows how an appreciation of the politics of the times provides an alternative interpretation of Shakespeare's motives and his awareness of the sensitivity of the moment.

He points out that Shakespeare invents (rather than lifting straight from history) a scene in which an angry mob mistakes Cinna the Poet for a conspiring politician and hacks him to death:

> It's hard not to conclude that the haze of Elizabethan censorship hanging in the air at this time seeps into the play at such moments; but it's also hard not to wonder at how little sympathy Shakespeare shows either for Cinna the Poet or for the other writer who appears in the play and gets caught in the maw of politics, the unnamed poet who tries to insert himself into the political action by attempting to reconcile the feuding Brutus and Cassius ... The message seems to be that it's a wise poet who knows his place and time, who doesn't go looking for trouble in a dangerous political world.

Shapiro adds that an awareness of the Elizabethan way of thinking, as well as of the way Shakespeare worked, explains the playwright's choice and the structure of the play. He acknowledges that opting to depict the assassination of a ruler was a daring decision but that his choice of Plutarch as a source was a 'careful and canny one'. Plutarch had been overlooked by many of Shakespeare's contemporaries and, more importantly, he knew that the Queen had translated Plutarch's *On Curiosity* and that Plutarch was 'at heart a monarchist'. Shapiro points out that the play was named after Caesar, even though he only appears in a few scenes, rather than Brutus.

However noble Brutus' motives, however morally and politically justified his actions, it would have been clear to many in Shakespeare's audience that he hadn't thought things through. Critics who fault *Julius Caesar* for being a broken-backed play, who are disappointed by the final two acts and who feel that the assassination takes place too early in the action, fail to understand that the two parts of the play – the events leading up to the assassination and the bloody civil strife that follow – go hand in hand. Even as Shakespeare offers compelling arguments for tyrannicide in the opening acts of the play, he shows in the closing ones the savage blood-letting and political breakdown that, if the English history he had so compellingly chronicled was any example, were sure to follow.

Group biographies

Other biographers have broken away from traditional structures by writing about a group or pair of writers whose lives and work are inextricably linked. This would seem most logical when dealing with siblings, especially if more than one was a writer – as in the case of the Brontës and, partially, the Mitfords. The biographer only has to explain their childhood and background once and each life should help to illuminate the others.

Recent accounts of the lives of the Mitford family have focused on this approach. The seven children of the 2nd Baron Redesdale – six girls and a boy who was killed in the Second World War – became famous for a variety of reasons. Deborah and her husband inherited Chatsworth stately home, Diana married the British Fascist Oswald Mosley and Unity became friendly with Hitler. Jessica Mitford (1917–1996) wrote an account of her eccentric early life in *Hons and Rebels* (1960), while her later work focused on investigative journalism. Her sister Nancy Mitford (1904–1973) wrote several highly autobiographical novels such as *The Pursuit of Love* (1945) and its sequel, *Love in a Cold Climate* (1949). Of the sisters, only Pamela led a quiet life.

More than one biographer has chosen to fold the sisters' story into a single account. Letters between them have also been published in a single volume: *Mitfords: Letters Between Six Sisters* (2007). Charlotte Mosley, daughter-in-law of Diana Mitford, edited this collection and another of letters between Nancy and her friend and fellow novelist, Evelyn Waugh.

▶ What challenges might the biographer face in telling, in one book, the lives of a group of six sisters, who held quite different views and possessed different talents? What do you think are the advantages of collecting together both sides of a correspondence, for example, between Vita Sackville-West and Virginia Woolf?

Another approach is to link the lives of a group of men and women through one event. This is what Richard Davenport-Hines did in *A Night at the Majestic* (2006), which tells the story of a famous dinner party at the Majestic Hotel in Paris in 1922, attended by the Russian composer Igor Stravinsky, the Irish writer James Joyce, the Russian dance impresario Sergei Diaghilev, the Spanish painter Pablo Picasso and Marcel Proust, author of *À La Recherche du Temps Perdu* (*Remembrance of Things Past*). It was the only time Proust and Joyce ever met and the occasion promised much. But, although the idea for the book seems like a clever one, many reviewers felt that it was perhaps too clever for its own good. Like many disappointing dinner parties, the act of bringing together a group of people served to diminish rather than multiply their individual wit and insight. Reports of the conversations vary – in one Proust and Joyce discuss their physical ailments; in another they claim not to have read each other's books. An examination of Proust's life is sandwiched between descriptions of the dinner party that begin and end the book. Significantly, the book was retitled *Proust at the Majestic* when it was published in America.

The Silent Woman: Plath and Hughes

Examining the work and lives of Ted Hughes and Sylvia Plath in one volume seems more logical and enlightening: after all it is impossible to assess the work of either without knowledge of their life together. But *The Silent Woman: Sylvia Plath and Ted Hughes* by Janet Malcolm (1994) is more than a joint biography. In it she explores the nature and ethics of biography and how lives can become mythologised and distorted after a writer's death. Malcolm sets out to track down as many of the characters who have played a part in constructing the various personae of Plath as she can, from biographers such as Anne Stevenson (author of the much criticised *Bitter Fame*, 1989), writers of memoirs like A. Alvarez (the poetry editor of *The Observer* newspaper who had been one of the first to recognise Plath's talent) to Trevor Thomas, who lived in a flat below Plath and may have been the last to see her alive.

Malcolm tests the main sources used by the biographer – letters, journals, memoir, literary works, and oral testimonies – to see how each can be found wanting. She starts by pointing out that Ted Hughes wrote two versions of his foreword to *The Journals of Sylvia Plath*, a selection of diary entries between 1950 and 1962, and examines how each differs. In particular, she looks at the way in which Hughes deals with his admission that he destroyed one of his wife's journals. She points out that in the later version, 'he has himself disappeared: "I destroyed" now becomes "her husband destroyed". Hughes can no longer sustain the fiction– on which all autobiographical writing is poised – that the person writing and the person being written about are a single seamless entity.'

But Malcolm is honest enough to acknowledge that she too has fallen prey to the sort of misinterpretation that can instantly transform someone's reputation.

In a postscript at the end of the British edition, she reveals how she read a note scribbled by Plath's mother, Aurelia, on one of Ted Hughes' letters which seemed to suggest that he had bought a house, which he had clearly not. There was one word that she had been unable to read. When she phoned the librarian at the Lilly Library where the letter is kept the librarian was able to decipher the word Malcolm found illegible: 'Ted *never* bought the property.'

▶ In the extract in Part 3 (page 93) Malcolm is highly visible. What are the advantages and disadvantages of this approach? What do the quotations from Plath and Alvarez, and the dialogue between Olwyn Hughes and Malcolm add to the description?

New perspectives: 'Was Jane Austen gay?'

Biographers may decide to approach their subject by stressing a completely new interpretation or by interpreting their life from a new angle. Sometimes, however, that interpretation can become distorted by publishers or by the press. When Terry Castle, Professor of English at Stanford University, reviewed a newly annotated edition of Jane Austen's letters in the *London Review of Books* (August, 1995), she suggested that Austen's closest relationship was with her sister, Cassandra. The magazine ran the article under the headline, 'Was Jane Austen gay?' Castle was inundated with telephone calls from newspapers, news agencies and television programmes demanding that she expand on Austen's sexuality. She eventually issued a statement through Stanford University News Service in which she put the record straight: 'Nowhere in my essay did I state that Jane Austen was a "lesbian" – certainly not in the modern clinical sense of the word – or that she had sex of some sort with her sister.' In a second statement she added:

> Social historians have been writing for the past twenty years about the profoundly homosocial nature of middle and upper-class English cultural life in the 18th and 19th centuries: the sexes were highly segregated, and powerful emotional (and sometimes physical) ties between persons of the same sex were both common in the period and often expressed in highly romantic or passionate terms. Unmarried women, especially siblings, frequently shared a bed – as Austen and Cassandra did for all of their adult lives. I have been accused of 'not realising' that such physical intimacy between women was in fact 'normal' or 'common' in the period, when that was precisely part of my point.

Castle believed that part of the misunderstanding arose from journalists' perception of her: since she was from San Francisco, they expected her to take a risqué approach to her subject and not to understand that women often shared a bed because England was so cold. Ironically, Castle had spent her childhood in Britain.

► In defending her review Castle claimed that many readers 'fetishise' Jane Austen and see her as a symbol of purity. Modern film adaptations of Austen's books have portrayed her world as one of rural charm. Is there anything wrong with these different interpretations (stressing the rural setting and her purity) of the same writer?

New perspectives: *Mrs Woolf and the Servants*

Like Jane Austen, Virginia Woolf's life has been interpreted in several different ways. Alison Light's book, *Mrs Woolf and the Servants* (2007), manages to find a fresh view of a writer who has been endlessly examined. Light's aim was to look at the conflict between the argument Woolf puts forward in *A Room of One's Own* for more writing about the lives of obscure women, like cleaners, and her private complaints about the 'servant question' to be found in her letters and diaries.

In an extract from *Sketch of the Past* (which Light uses to introduce Part Four of her book) Woolf says:

> Consider what immense forces society brings to play on each of us, how that society changes from decade to decade; and also from class to class; well, if we cannot analyse these invisible presences, we know very little of the subject of the memoir; and again how futile life-writing becomes. I see myself as a fish in a stream; deflected; held in place; but cannot describe the stream.

An analysis of her novels shows that she has great difficulty in describing men and women from a lower class. (See the extract from *Mrs Woolf and the Servants* in Part 3, page 92.) As well as offering a different perspective on Woolf, Light's book weaves in a social history of domestic service: the fact, for example, that even servants' beds were inferior – two feet six inches wide, rather than the standard three feet. Light faced the problem of the wealth of material about Woolf compared with a dearth of material about the actual servants: just a few photos and a handful of letters. She structures her book by dividing it into chapters about Woolf and her relationship with various servants, and has inserted fictionalised sections in italics at the beginning of each section.

Other forms of life writing

Letters and diaries

Literary biographies, by the very nature of their subject, are likely to rely more on letters than other types of biography. In *The Silent Woman* Janet Malcolm says:

> Letters are the great fixative of experience. Time erodes feeling. Time creates indifference. Letters prove to us that we once cared. They are the fossils of feeling. This is why biographers prize them so: they are

biography's only conduit to unmediated experience. Everything else the biographer touches is stale, hashed over, told and retold, dubious, unauthentic, suspect. Only when he reads a subject's letters does the biographer feel he has come fully into his presence, and only when he quotes from the letters does he share with his readers his sense of life retrieved. And he shares something else: the feeling of transgression that comes from reading letters not meant for one's eyes.

▶ Do you agree and do you think this is true of all letters? The conventions and habit of letter writing have changed dramatically over the past few centuries. Should future biographers treat the letters written by today's famous authors differently from letters written a century ago?

Malcolm describes a diary entry for 1958 when Plath talks about a fight she had because Hughes was with another woman when they were living in Boston as 'one of the great novelistic set pieces of *The Journal* … the shaped, premeditated work of a writerly narrator, rather than the innocent blurtings of a diarist …'. But she goes on to say that later interpretations of whether or not Hughes was actually unfaithful are bound to be flawed:

> In a work of non fiction we almost never know the truth of what happened. The ideal of unmediated reporting is regularly achieved only in fiction, where the writer faithfully reports on what is going on in his imagination.

▶ In *Testament of Youth* Vera Brittain uses a variety of different sources, including letters and her own poems. As a biographer would you rather read the letters Brittain chose to make public or the unpublished letters? Why?

Autobiographical fiction

Many novelists dislike the tag, 'autobiographical fiction' – perhaps because they see it as an implied criticism: that they do not have the imagination to invent an original plot but, instead, are forced to excavate their own life history. Clearly, some fiction is more autobiographical than others. For Virginia Woolf the line between fiction and autobiographical writings remained fine, if not blurred. For other writers their own life has provided no more than inspiration or ways in which they can authenticate an experience.

In *Small Island* two key characters, Gilbert and Hortense, like the author's own parents, were born in Jamaica and emigrated to Britain in 1948. Also like the author's parents, they witnessed how Britons who had lived in the country for more than a generation reacted to the arrivals. There may be other similarities, but beyond these bare facts the novel has a life very much of its own.

Zadie Smith is keen to play down any comparisons between her own life and her comic novel, *White Teeth*. The novel is set in Willesden, a part of North London where she grew up. In the novel Clara was, like one of Smith's parents, born in Jamaica and marries a white man, Archie. But in an interview on her publisher's website Smith points out that, unlike Clara's daughter, Irie, she is not an only child. In answer to the question, 'Are there any echoes of your family in the novel?' she replies:

> Nope ... I'm extremely close to my younger brothers; family is everything and that's why none of my family appear in *White Teeth* in any obvious way. The people in the book are fairly savage to each other. My family are a much happier, calmer unit than Archie's. The Smiths could never keep up with the Joneses.
> (See: www.randomhouse.com/boldtype/0700/smith/interview.html)

▶ Do you think authors are necessarily best placed to judge the extent to which their work is autobiographical or not?

The influence of Freud and increased emphasis on individual experience has led some readers to concentrate on the bald facts of an author's life when interpreting their work. Literary biography aims to show how a writer's life might inform their work but also to examine how other influences shape it. This might include the time in which they wrote, and the thinkers and authors they associated with or read.

Take for example the American writer Kurt Vonnegut (1922–2007). Anyone researching his life would quickly discover several facts that seem to explain the underlying pessimism in many of his books. His German–American parents ran a brewing business in America that was hit first by anti-German feeling after the First World War and then by the prohibition of alcohol in the 1920s. Vonnegut's mother failed to have any of her short stories published and on Mother's Day 1944 took a fatal overdose. Towards the end of the war Vonnegut, who had enlisted in the army, was captured by the Germans and forced to work in a factory at Dresden. Here, in February 1945, he experienced the massive aerial bombardment by American and British bombers, which caused the infamous firestorms that killed an estimated thirty-five thousands civilians in two hours. He took shelter in a subterranean meat store called Schlachthof Fünf (Slaughterhouse Five) and emerged to find a flattened city in which he was put to work clearing bodies.

Nearly twenty-five years and seven novels later he used this experience as the premise for his most famous novel, *Slaughterhouse Five or, The Children's Crusade: A duty-dance with death* (1969). But in interviews he makes light of the lasting influence of Dresden in his work. Many critics have pointed out that the political backdrop against which he wrote – the war in Vietnam, the Russian invasion of Czechoslovakia, the civil rights struggle in America and student riots in Paris – was just as significant as Vonnegut's wartime experience. A passage towards the end of *Slaughterhouse Five* suggests other contemporaneous influences:

Robert Kennedy, whose summer home is eight miles from the home I live in all year round, was shot two nights ago. He died last night. So it goes.

Martin Luther King was shot a month ago. He died, too. So it goes. And every day my Government gives me a count of corpses created by military science in Vietnam. So it goes.

My father died many years ago now – of natural causes. So it goes. He was a sweet man. He was a gun nut, too. He left me his guns. They rust.

There can also be the temptation to confuse an author's views with the views of their characters. This is exactly what happened in Ian McEwan's novel, *Saturday*, which is set on the day that a million people marched through London to protest at the Iraq war. In a newspaper interview McEwan explained his ambivalence towards the conflict: he could not help feeling relief at the removal of a dictator, but he experienced unease about the invasion of a country by a foreign force. He used these conflicting feelings to write an argument between *Saturday*'s main character, a neurosurgeon called Henry Perowne, and his daughter. But the scene caused confusion among some readers:

I was able to draw on everything that I felt – everything she said I could believe, and everything he said – almost everything – I could at least understand. And I also knew that the more popular thing would be to write a novel in which Henry Perowne was really against the war, would be a right-on guy, and not take private patients – but why do that? I wanted him to be a little more awkward to the reader. But I mean, a lot of readers, they just thought Henry Perowne was me.

(*Guardian*, 18 August 2007)

▶ Look at the extract from an interview by Zadie Smith, author of *White Teeth*, with Ian McEwan (Part 3, page 101). What does this reveal about the extent to which authors use their own circumstances in their writing? In what ways is this interview different because it is conducted by a fellow novelist, rather than a journalist?

The value and use of sources

Every biographer dreams of finding a new stash of letters that no one else has read or some other fresh source that has yet to be tapped. But the way that the biographer interprets their findings is as telling as the sources themselves. Charles Nicholl's *The Lodger: Shakespeare on Silver Street* (2007), for example, uses a document that was first discovered nearly a century before to build a compelling new view of Shakespeare.

Official sources

Biographers usually view official documents, such as birth, marriage and death certificates, wills and divorce papers, as among their more reliable sources. However, even these are only as truthful as the people supplying the information and the officials who record it. Brides lie about their ages, civil servants trip over the spellings of surnames or reflect the prejudices and sensibilities of their age when deciding which facts to include.

The national census, which started in 1801 and which has been held every ten years – with the exception of 1941 when the Second World War intervened – offers insights into people living in England and Wales. An entry from the 1871 census, for example, provides a snapshot of the life of George Eliot (1819–1880) whose real name was Mary Anne Evans and who was the author of books such as *The Mill on the Floss* (1860), *Silas Marner* (1861) and *Middlemarch* (1871). The entry can be found at: www.nationalarchives.gov.uk/news/stories/georgeeliot-popup.htm

The entry states that George H. Lewes is head of the household, living with his wife, Marian, in London. But it is misleading. Although Evans and Lewes lived together for over twenty years, she was never his wife and while the census leaves her occupation blank, Lewes' is described as 'literature'.

▶ Despite its omissions, in what ways could this census entry be useful to George Eliot's biographer?

Oral testimony

Biographers who choose to write about recent authors or poets have the advantage of talking to men and women who knew them and, if they are still alive, to the writer themselves, as Mrs Gaskell and James Boswell both did. Zadie Smith's interview with Ian McEwan (see Part 3, page 101) shows the value of the author's insight into his own work.

In 1965 a journalist from *The Sunday Times Magazine* tracked down the real Miss Joan Hunter Dunn, who is the focal point for the poem by Sir John Betjeman (1906–1984), 'A Subaltern's Love Song':

> Miss J. Hunter Dunn, Miss J. Hunter Dunn,
> Furnish'd and burnish'd by Aldershot sun,
> What strenuous singles we played after tea,
> We in the tournament – you against me!

The poem displays a nostalgia for a certain type of suburban Englishness and Miss J. Hunter Dunn was widely believed to be a creation of the poet's imagination. Later Betjeman revealed that he had worshipped her from afar when she was the deputy-catering manager at the Ministry of Information where he worked during the Second World War. Joan Hunter Dunn told *The Sunday Times* journalist that Betjeman had taken her out to lunch in February 1941 but that they were never lovers. When the poet told her that 'A Subaltern's Love Song' was about her, she pointed out that she came from Farnborough in Hampshire, not Aldershot. Betjeman later told the reporter that this was near enough to Aldershot not to matter.

▶ Does the knowledge that Miss J. Hunter Dunn was a real person add anything to the appreciation of the poem and the way that Betjeman worked?

Illustrations

Photos, sketches and paintings can provide clues to a writer's social status, their friends and the image that they hoped to convey. Publishers believe that an author photo can also influence a book's success. But if a writer becomes closely associated with one image it can affect future reactions to their work and lead to misconceptions about their personality.

Only two authentic portraits of Shakespeare exist and both were produced after his death. As James Shapiro says in *1599*:

> The overwhelming desire for a more expressive Shakespeare, a truer portrait of the artist, explains why paintings of impostors who more closely resemble the Shakespeare of our imagination now hang in the National Portrait Gallery and elsewhere and are the ones we find reproduced on everything from coffee mugs to editions of his work.

In 2007 Wordsworth Editions published new versions of Jane Austen's novels which carried a startlingly different portrait of the author. The publishers had adapted the familiar image, painted by Jane's sister, Cassandra: her cap was removed to reveal tumbling curls, her lips and cheeks were given a hint of colour and her chest made more pronounced. This reinvention led to a wave of controversy. One critic pointed out that this modern 'make-over' did Austen a disservice: in reality she was not so obviously attractive, she never married and her novels deal with whether a good heart or a pretty face are more likely to win over a man.

Kathryn Hughes faced a similar dilemma in her acclaimed biography of George Eliot. Several of Eliot's contemporaries described her as ugly, but Hughes' publishers demanded that the biography's cover should carry the most flattering image of Eliot – and even this was 'touched up'. A few readers wrote to point out that Eliot's awareness of her own physical shortcomings played a strong part in the motivation behind her work. As Hughes acknowledged, it was Eliot's awareness of what appearance means that led her to create such vivid characters as Maggie Tulliver in *The Mill on the Floss* (1860) and the vain Hetty Sorrel in *Adam Bede* (1859).

▶ Consider the cover of a biography you know well. What image do you think the publishers are trying to convey?

The structure of a biography depends on several factors: the availability and scope of sources and how the biographer chooses to use them, the pattern of the subject's life and when they produced their work, and the prejudices and preferences of the biographer. The publisher and the market the biographer is aiming at will also have an effect on the style and format of the biography. The texts and extracts that follow in Part 3 show just how varied life writing can be.

Assignments

1 Think carefully about a literary biography you have read recently. In what order does the biographer tell the story of their subject's life? If you had to start the biography at a different point in their life which would you choose and why? How does the biographer relate the author's life to their literary output?

2 Look closely at the range of sources used in a particular literary biography. Does the biographer make greater use of some, rather than others? How will the sources used by future biographers of novelists and poets writing today differ from a biographer writing in the 20th century?

3 In 1953 Evelyn Waugh, who wrote novels such as *Scoop*, *Brideshead Revisited* and *A Handful of Dust*, was interviewed for a radio programme called *Frankly Speaking*. Waugh later fictionalised the often acerbic exchanges in *The Ordeal of Gilbert Pinfold* (1957). Read the novel and then listen to the interview (*The Spoken Word: Evelyn Waugh*, British Library, ISBN 978 0 7123 0546 4). How does your awareness of Waugh's radio experience affect your appreciation of the novel?

4 Compare the extracts in Part 3 (pages 80 and 81) from J.G. Ballard's novel *Empire of the Sun* (1984) and his autobiography, *Miracles of Life, Shanghai to Shepperton* (2008). In what ways would you say that the novel is autobiographical? How is the style of *Miracles of Life* different?

Texts and extracts

The texts and extracts that follow have been chosen to illustrate key themes and points made elsewhere in the book, and to provide material which may be useful when working on the tasks and assignments. As far as possible, space has been given to texts and extracts which are not so readily available elsewhere. The items are arranged alphabetically by author.

Peter Ackroyd

From *Dickens* (1990)

Ackroyd was already an established critic, poet, novelist and biographer when he wrote his controversial life of Dickens. The book includes several deviations from the main story of Dickens' life. This second imaginary encounter between biographer and subject appears about two thirds of the way into the biography.

We were sitting in the Mid-Victorian Room of the Geffrye Museum. It was late at night, and the staff had all departed. Dickens got up from his chair, and started touching or rearranging the small domestic objects which had been placed within the interior for the purposes of authenticity. He was humming the old song, 'Long time I courted you, Miss ...' He sat down after a few moments, and adjusted the crease in his blue serge trousers: I noticed the stripe of dark satin running down both sides. 'You just said now that you understood me,' he went on as if we had not stopped talking. 'But I don't think that you do. How could you understand me when I do not even understand myself?'

'The biographer –'

'– Oh, biographers. Biographers are simply novelists without imagination!' He looked across at me with that full, direct glance which I had come to know so well; and then he smiled. 'Forgive me. As I said, I am tired. And some of my best friends are biographers.'

'When you say that you do not understand yourself, do you mean that you don't care to?'

He snatched at the word. 'And there's another thing. I never really know what I *mean*. That is the question I can never bring myself to ask anyone when they talk about my writing. But what does it mean? What does it mean?'

'What does a novel mean? It *means* only that you have managed to complete it.'

He laughed. 'Yes. Very good. And that, after all, is the principal matter. Tell me more about myself.'

'You are nervous, although you try not to show it. You are proud, although you pretend not to be –'

'But I am the least arrogant of men. And as for nerves –.' He was turning his signet ring around and around upon his finger.

'You see people so clearly, and yet really you never see them at all.'

'Are you saying that I live in a world of my own devising?' He gave me a quick, funny glance.

'Actually, I don't know. I'm making all this up.'

Now he laughed out loud. 'Precisely. You know as little about me as I do. But the important thing, upon which we are agreed, is that you should finish your work. And it is in the very act of completion that some new truth will be revealed.'

'And, when your own career upon earth is over, will the truth of your life also be revealed?'

'Let us not talk of that. Let us not discuss dying. I am not concerned with myself, you understand, but with the books that will remain unwritten and the characters who will stay unborn. I have so many of them in my head, you know, I *see* so many of them in front of me – what will happen to them if they cannot come into the world? Will they migrate to the imaginations of other writers? Yes, that is it. Like transported criminals they will find a new world. Perhaps in centuries to come…' He got up from his chair in order to wander along the narrow corridor which connected the rooms of various periods in this museum; he turned to his right and walked past the interiors of the eighteenth and seventeenth centuries; then he retraced his steps, passed me, and stopped to consider the bakelite wireless and the linoleum flooring of the Thirties Room. He walked up to the edge of this exhibit and seemed about to enter the room itself, but then he checked himself; he did not want to cross the threshold. Instead he came back to the mid-Victorian interior, where I was waiting for him. He picked up a small jar containing lavender. Then he laughed, and put it down again. 'The mystery is too deep to fathom.'

'The mystery of time?'

'No, no.' Charles Dickens laughed again. 'The mystery of my own self.' Dawn was breaking when I left him.

Maya Angelou

From *I Know Why The Caged Bird Sings* (1970)

The prologue to *I Know Why The Caged Bird Sings*, the first volume of Angelou's autobiography, sets the scene for her account of growing up in a poor black community in racially segregated Arkansas. Angelou, who is also a poet and performer, has spent her life fighting for racial and sexual equality.

'What you looking at me for?
I didn't come to stay …'

I hadn't so much forgot as I couldn't bring myself to remember. Other things were more important.

'What you looking at me for?

I didn't come to stay …'

Whether I could remember the rest of the poem or not was immaterial. The truth of the statement was like a wadded-up handkerchief, sopping wet in my fists, and the sooner they accepted it the quicker I could let my hands open and the air would cool my palms.

'What you looking at me for …?'

The children's section of the Colored Methodist Episcopal Church was wiggling and giggling over my well-known forgetfulness.

The dress I wore was lavender taffeta, and each time I breathed it rustled, and now that I was sucking in air to breathe out shame it sounded like crepe paper on the back of hearses.

As I'd watched Momma put ruffles on the hem and cute little tucks around the waist, I knew that once I put it on I'd look like a movie star. (It was silk and that made up for the awful color.) I was going to look like one of the sweet little white girls who were everybody's dream of what was right with the world. Hanging softly over the black Singer sewing machine, it looked like magic, and when people saw me wearing it they were going to run up to me and say, 'Marguerite (sometimes it was 'dear Marguerite'), forgive us, please, we didn't know who you were,' and I would answer generously, 'No, you couldn't have known. Of course I forgive you.'

Just thinking about it made me go around with angel's dust sprinkled over my face for days. But Easter's early morning sun had shown the dress to be a plain ugly cut-down from a white woman's once-was-purple throwaway. It was old-lady-long too, but it didn't hide my skinny legs, which had been greased with Blue Seal Vaseline and powdered with the Arkansas red clay. The age-faded color made my skin look dirty like mud, and everyone in church was looking at my skinny legs.

Wouldn't they be surprised when one day I woke out of my black ugly dream, and my real hair, which was long and blond, would take the place of the kinky mass that Momma wouldn't let me straighten? My light-blue eyes were going to hypnotise them, after all the things they said about 'my daddy must of been a Chinaman' (I thought they meant made out of china, like a cup) because my eyes were so small and squinty. Then they would understand why I had never picked up a Southern accent, or spoke the common slang, and why I had to be forced to eat pigs' tails and snouts. Because I was really white and because a cruel fairy stepmother, who was understandably jealous of my beauty, had turned me into a too-big Negro girl, with nappy black hair, broad feet and a space between her teeth that would hold a number-two pencil.

'What you looking ...' The minister's wife leaned toward me, her long yellow face full of sorry. She whispered, 'I just come to tell you, it's Easter Day.' I repeated, jamming the words together, 'Ijustcome totellyouit'sEasterDay,' as low as possible. The giggles hung in the air like melting clouds that were waiting to rain on me. I held up two fingers, close to my chest, which meant that I had to go to the toilet, and tiptoed toward the rear of the church. Dimly, somewhere over my head, I heard ladies saying, 'Lord bless the child,' and 'Praise God.' My head was up and my eyes were open, but I didn't see anything. Halfway down the aisle, the church exploded with 'Were you there when they crucified my Lord?' and I tripped over a foot stuck out from the children's pew. I stumbled and started to say something, or maybe to scream, but a green persimmon, or it could have been a lemon, caught me between the legs and squeezed. I tasted the sour on my tongue and felt it in the back of my mouth. Then before I reached the door, the sting was burning down my legs and into my Sunday socks. I tried to hold, to squeeze it back, to keep it from speeding, but when I reached the church porch I knew I'd have to let it go, or it would probably run right back up to my head and my poor head would burst like a dropped watermelon, and all the brains and spit and tongue and eyes would roll all over the place. So I ran down into the yard and let it go. I ran, peeing and crying, not toward the toilet out back but to our house. I'd get a whipping for it, to be sure, and the nasty children would have something new to tease me about. I laughed anyway, partially for the sweet release; still, the greater joy came not only from being liberated from the silly church but from the knowledge that I wouldn't die from a busted head.

If growing up is painful for the Southern Black girl, being aware of her displacement is the rust on the razor that threatens the throat.

It is an unnecessary insult.

John Aubrey

From *Brief Lives* (1813)

In this extract Aubrey sketches the life of William Shakespeare in a style that is typically rumbustious and which also shows his sometimes casual attitude to accuracy. He seems to be referring to Dogberry but the night constable appears in *Much Ado About Nothing*, not *Midsummer Night's Dream*.

MR WILLIAM SHAKESPEARE was borne at Stratford upon Avon in the County of Warwick. His father was a Butcher, and I have been told heretofore by some of the neighbours, that when he was a boy he exercised his father's Trade, but when he kill'd a Calfe, he would doe it in a high style, and make a Speech. There was at that time another Butcher's son in this Towne, that was held not at all inferior to him for a naturall witt, his acquaintance and coetanean, but dyed young.

This William being naturally inclined to Poetry and acting, came to London, I guesse, about eighteen. And was an Actor at one of the Play-houses, and did act exceedingly well: now Ben Johnson was never a good Actor, but an excellent Instructor.

He began early to make essayes at Dramatique Poetry, which at that time was very lowe; and his Plays tooke well. He was a handsome well shap't man: very good company, and of a very readie and pleasant smooth Witt.

The Humour of the Constable, in *Midsomernight's Dreame* he happened to take at Grendon in Bucks which is the roade from London to Stratford and there was living that Constable about 1642 when I first came to Oxon: Mr Josias Howe is of that parish, and knew him. Ben Johnson and he did gather Humours of men dayly where ever they came.

One time as he was at the Tavern at Stratford super Avon, one Combes an old rich Usurer was to be buryed, he makes there this extemporary Eitaph,

> *Ten in the Hundred the Devill allowes,*
> *But Combes will have twelve, he swears and vowes:*
> *If any one askes who lies in this Tombe,*
> *'Hoh!' quoth the Devill, ''Tis my John o-Combe.'*

He was wont to goe into his native Countrey once a yeare. I thinke I have been told that he left two or three hundred pounds per annum there and thereabout: to a sister.

I have heard Sir William Davenant and Mr Thomas Shadwell (who is counted the best Comoedian we have now) say, that he had the most prodigious Witt, and did admire his naturall parts beyond all other Dramaticall writers. He was wont to say, That he never blotted out a line in his Life: sayd Ben Johnson, 'I wish he had blotted-out a thousand.

His Comoedies will remaine witt, as long as the English tongue is understood: for that he handles *mores hominum* [human nature]; now our present writers reflect so much upon particular persons, and coxcombeities, that twenty yeares hence, they will not be understood.

Though as Ben Johnson sayes of him, that he had but little Latin, and lesse Greek; He understood Latine pretty well: for he had been in his younger yeares a Schoolmaster in the Countrey.

J.G. Ballard

From *Empire of the Sun* (1984) and *Miracles of Life: Shanghai to Shepperton* (2008)

In the 1960s J.G. Ballard (1930–2009) became known as a science fiction writer, particularly of controversial novels such as *Crash* (1973) in which he explored the eroticism of a car accident. His work became more widely known when Steven Spielberg directed a film of his novel, *Empire of the Sun*, in 1987. Both this and his autobiography, *Miracles of Life*, describe his experiences as a boy ('Jim' in the fictional account) held in a Japanese internment camp during the Second World War. In these two extracts – one written twenty years after the other – Ballard describes a beggar who lived near their house in the comfortable European community that existed before the Japanese invasion. The first extract is from *Empire of the Sun*.

Pierrot and pirate, his parents sat silently as they set off for Hungjao, a country district five miles to the west of Shanghai. Usually his mother would caution Yang to avoid the old beggar who lay at the end of the drive. But as Yang swung the heavy car through the gates, barely pausing before he accelerated along Amherst Avenue, Jim saw that the front wheel had crushed the man's foot. This beggar had arrived two months earlier, a bundle of living rags whose only possessions were a frayed paper mat and an empty Craven A tin which he shook at passers-by. He never moved from the mat, but ferociously defended his plot outside the taipan's gates. Even Boy and Number One Coolie, the houseboy and the chief scullion, had been unable to shift him.

However, the position had brought the old man little benefit. There were hard times in Shanghai that winter, and after a week-long cold spell he was too tired to raise his tin. Jim worried about the beggar, and his mother told him that Coolie had taken a bowl of rice to him. After a heavy snowfall one night in early December the snow formed a thick quilt from which the old man's face emerged like a sleeping child's above an eiderdown. Jim told himself that he never moved because he was warm under the snow.

There were so many beggars in Shanghai. Along Amherst Avenue they sat outside the gates of the houses, shaking their Craven A tins like reformed smokers. Many displayed lurid wounds and deformities, but no one noticed them that afternoon. Refugees from the towns and villages around Shanghai were pouring into the city. Wooden carts and rickshaws crowded Amherst Avenue, each loaded with a peasant family's entire possessions. Adults and children bent under the bales strapped to their backs, forcing the wheels with their hands. Rickshaw coolies hauled at their shafts, chanting and spitting, veins as thick as fingers clenched into the meat of their swollen calves. Petty clerks pushed bicycles loaded with mattresses, charcoal stoves and sacks of rice. A legless beggar, his thorax strapped into a huge leather shoe, swung himself along the road through the maze of wheels, a wooden dumb-bell in each hand. He spat and swiped at the Packard when Yang tried to force him out of the car's way, and then vanished among the wheels of the pedicabs and rickshaws, confident in his kingdom of saliva and dust.

****

Jim waited in the front seat of the Packard while his parents changed and their suitcases were loaded into the trunk. When they set off through the gates he looked down at the motionless figure of the beggar on his frayed mat. He could see the pattern of the Packard's Firestone tyres in the old man's left foot. Leaves and shreds of newspaper covered his head, and already he was becoming part of the formless rubbish from which he had emerged.

Jim felt sorry for the old beggar, but for some reason he could think only of the tyre patterns in his foot. If they had been driving in Mr Maxted's Studebaker the pattern would have been different: the old man would have been stamped with the imprint of the Goodyear Company ...

From *Miracles of Life*

As a small boy aged five or six I must have accepted all this without a thought, along with the backbreaking labour of the coolies unloading the ships along the Bund, middle-aged men with bursting calf veins, swaying and sighing under enormous loads slung from their shoulder-yokes, moving a slow step at a time towards the nearby godowns, the large warehouses of the Chinese merchants. Afterwards they would squat with a bowl of rice and a cabbage leaf that somehow gave them the energy to bear these monstrous loads. In the Nanking Road the Chinese begging boys ran after our car and tapped the windows, crying 'No mama, no papa, no whisky soda ...' Had they picked up the cry thrown back at them ironically by Europeans who didn't care?

When I was six, before the Japanese invasion in 1937, an old beggar sat down with his back to the wall at the foot of our drive, at the point where our car passed before turning into Amherst Avenue. I looked at him from the rear seat of our Buick, a thin, ancient man dressed in rags, undernourished all his life and now taking his last breaths. He rattled a Craven A tin at passers-by, but no one gave him anything. After a few days he was visibly weaker, and I asked my mother if No. 2 Coolie would take the old man a little food. Tired of my pestering, she eventually gave in, and said that Coolie would take the old man a bowl of soup. The next day it snowed, and the old man was covered with a white quilt. I remember telling myself that he would feel warmer under this soft eiderdown. He stayed there, under his quilt, for several days, and then he was gone.

Forty years later I asked my mother why we had not fed this old man at the bottom of our drive, and she replied, 'If we had fed him, within two hours there would have been fifty beggars there.' In her way, she was right. Enterprising Europeans had brought immense prosperity to Shanghai, but even Shanghai's wealth could never feed the millions of destitute Chinese driven towards the city by war and famine. I still think of that old man, of a human being reduced to such a desperate end a few yards from where I slept in a warm bedroom surrounded by my expensive German toys. But as a boy I was easily satisfied by a small act of kindness, a notional bowl of soup that I probably knew at the time was no more than a phrase on my mother's lips. By the time I was fourteen I had become as fatalistic about death, poverty and hunger as the Chinese. I knew that kindness alone would feed few mouths and save no lives.

Vera Brittain

From *Testament of Youth* (1933) and *Letters from a Lost Generation: First World War Letters of Vera Brittain and Four Friends* (1998)

In this extract from her autobiography Vera Brittain describes visiting the family home of her fiancé, Roland Leighton, after his death on 23 December 1915 and writing to her brother, Edward, about the experience. The second extract is a longer version of the letter, which was not published at the time.

From *Testament of Youth*

I had arrived at the cottage that morning to find his mother and sister standing in helpless distress in the midst of his returned kit, which was lying, just opened, all over the floor. The garments sent back included the outfit that he had been wearing when he was hit. I wondered, and I wonder still, why it was thought necessary to return such relics – the tunic torn back and front by the bullet, a khaki vest dark and stiff with blood, and a pair of blood-stained breeches slit open at the top by someone obviously in a violent hurry. Those gruesome rags made me realise, as I had never realised before, all that France really meant. Eighteen months afterwards the smell of Étaples village, though fainter and more diffused, brought back to me the memory of those poor remnants of patriotism.

'Everything,' I wrote later to Edward, 'was damp and worn and simply caked with mud. And I was glad that neither you nor Victor nor anyone who may some day go to the front was there to see. If you had been, you would have been overwhelmed by the horror of war without its glory. For though he had only worn the things when living, the smell of those clothes was the smell of graveyards and the Dead. The mud of France which covered them was not ordinary mud; it had not the usual clean pure smell of earth, but it was as though it were saturated with dead bodies – dead that had been dead a long, long time … There was his cap, bent in and shapeless out of recognition – the soft cap he wore rakishly on the back of his head – with the badge thickly coated with mud. He must have fallen on top of it, or perhaps one of the people who fetched him in trampled on it.'

Edward wrote gently and humbly in reply, characteristically emphasising the simple, less perturbing things that I had mentioned in another part of my letter.

'I expect he had only just received the box of cigarettes and the collars and braces I gave him for Christmas and I feel glad that he did get them because he must have thought of me then.'

So oppressively at length did the charnel-house smell pervade the small sitting-room, that Roland's mother turned desperately to her husband:

'Robert, take those clothes away into the kitchen and don't let me see them again: I must either burn or bury them. They smell of death; they are not Roland; they even seem to detract from his memory and spoil his glamour. I won't have anything more to do with them!'

What actually happened to the clothes I never knew, but, incongruously enough, it was amid this heap of horror and decay that we found, surrounded by torn bills and letters, the black manuscript note-book containing his poems. On the fly-leaf he had copied a few lines written by John Masefield on the subject of patriotism …

From *Letters from a Lost Generation*

All Roland's things had just been sent back from the front through Cox's; they had just opened them and they were all lying on the floor. I had no idea before of the after-results of an officer's death, or what the returned kit, of which so much has been written in the papers, really meant. It was terrible. Mrs Leighton and Clare were both crying as bitterly as on the day we heard of His death, and Mr Leighton with his usual instinct was taking all the things everybody else wanted & putting them where nobody could ever find them. (His doings always seem to me to supply the slight element of humour which makes tragedy so much more tragic.) There were His clothes – the clothes in which He came home from the front last time – another set rather less worn, and underclothing and accessories of various descriptions. Everything was damp & worn and simply caked with mud. And I was glad that neither you nor Victor nor anyone else who may some day go to the front was there to see. If you had been you would have been overwhelmed by the horror of war without its glory. For though he had only worn the things when living, the smell of those clothes was the smell of graveyards & the Dead. The mud of France which covered them was not ordinary mud; it had not the usual clean pure smell of earth, but it was as though it were saturated with dead bodies – dead that had been dead a long, long time. All the sepulchres and catacombs of Rome could not make me realise mortality and decay and corruption as vividly as did the smell of those clothes. I know now what he meant when he used to write of 'this refuse-heap of a country' or 'a trench that is nothing but a charnel-house'. And the wonder is, not that he temporally lost the extremest refinements of his personality as Mrs Leighton says he did, but that he ever kept any of it at all – let along nearly the whole. He was more marvellous than even I ever dreamed. There was his cap, bent in and shapeless out of recognition – the soft cap he wore rakishly on the back of his head – with the badge coated thickly with mud. He must have fallen on top of it, or perhaps one of the people who fetched him in trampled on it. The clothes he was wearing when wounded were those in which he came home last time. We discovered that the bullet was an expanding one. The hole where it went in in front – well below where the belt would have been, just beside the right-hand bottom pocket of the tunic – was almost microscopic, but at the back, almost exactly where his back bone would have been, there was quite a large rent. The under things he was wearing at the time have evidently had to be destroyed, but they sent back a khaki waistcoat or vest (whatever that garment is you wear immediately below your tunic in cold weather) which was dark and stiff with blood, and a pair of khaki breeches also in the same state, which had been slit open at the top by someone in a great hurry – probably the Doctor in haste to get at the wound, or perhaps even by one of the men. Even the tabs of his braces were blood-stained too. He must have fallen on his back as in every case the back of his clothes was much more stained & muddy than in front.

The charnel-house smell seemed to grow stronger and stronger till it pervaded the room and obliterated everything else. Finally Mrs Leighton said 'Robert, take those clothes away into the kitchen, and don't let me see them again; I must either burn or bury them. They smell of Death; they are not Roland, they even seem to detract from his memory & spoil his glamour. I won't have any more to do with them.' And indeed one could never imagine those things the same as those in which he had lived & walked. One couldn't believe anyone alive had been in them at all. No, they were not Him. So Mr Leighton took them away; they are going to keep only that blood-stained vest he was wounded in, if it can be sterilized, as I think it can – and his Sam Browne belt. After the clothes had gone we opened the window wide & felt better, but it was a long time before the smell and even the taste of them went away.

... Even all the little things had the same faint smell, and were damp & mouldy. The only things untouched by damp or mud or mould were my photograph, kept carefully in an envelope, and his leather cigarette case, with a few cigarettes, a tiny photo of his Mother & George Meredith & the three little snapshots Miss Bervon took of us, inside. He must have had those things always with him, and the warmth of his body overruled the damp & decay of everything. There was his haversack crammed full of letters – he seemed to keep all he received. I found the rest of mine, and also several of yours, which I return in this. I seized them at once; I thought you would like them because they had been close to him, and also Mr Leighton has a habit of regarding everybody's letters to Roland as public property, much the same as Father regards yours to other people. He would be quite capable of reading mine; I saw him carefully engrossed in some of Mrs Leighton's, much to her dismay, and he was handling one of Victor's in a suspicious manner ...

Then there was the box of cigarettes you gave him recently – opened & sampled but not much used – the socks Mother knitted him, the pen & pipe and book I gave him, and your present 'A Tall Ship'. Among his letters were one or two envelopes addressed to Mrs Leighton & me, having no letters inside. And there was one which interested me very much; it was from the same Father Purdie who has written to me lately. The one we found was written in the summer, before he came home on leave; it is about contributions & details for the 'Catholic Journal', and shows him to have [been] a confessed & acknowledged Roman Catholic all that time ago. But he never said anything to us about it when he was home. How reserved he was about some things! It reminds me of the small incident at Maldon of his showing you his fountain pen & not telling you it was from me. But I think he imagined I should have disapproved of his Roman Catholicism.

But, most important of all, a Book, a private exercise book, came back in his haversack containing some poems of his own, in various stages of completeness, mostly written in pencil, beside, which even 'Violets' does not stand out as the height of his achievement. Some of the poems, like 'Triolet' & 'Lines on a Picture by Herbert Schmaltz', we already know. But the others, apparently, he has never shown anybody. There are seven of them. They are mostly love-lyrics – and I read them with a queer inward exultation over what his death has revealed. He was always reserved – less so in his letters than in himself, but until I read these poems I think I never quite realised – I copied them all out. I don't think any were meant to be in their finished state, and transcription with some was quite difficult, there were so many substitutions & alternative expressions ...

Elizabeth Gaskell

From *The Life of Charlotte Brontë* (1857)

Mrs Gaskell was already the author of several successful novels such as *Cranford* (1853) when Charlotte Brontë's father asked her to write a biography of his daughter, who had died in 1855. He hoped the book would restore the family name after some critics had taken offence at the passionate nature of his daughters' novels, particularly *Jane Eyre*. Mrs Gaskell was determined to depict Charlotte's life as one of remoteness and drudgery that would go some way to explaining the coarseness of her books.

> Her life at Haworth was so unvaried that the postman's call was the event of her day. Yet she dreaded the great temptation of centring all her thoughts upon this one time, and losing her interest in the smaller hopes and employments of the remaining hours. Thus she conscientiously denied herself the pleasure of writing letters too frequently, because the answers (when she received them) took the flavour out of the rest of her life; or the disappointment, when the replies did not arrive, lessened her energy for her home duties.
>
> The winter of this year in the north was hard and cold; it affected Miss Brontë's health less than usual, however, probably because the change and the medical advice she had taken in London had done her good; probably, also, because her friend had come to pay her a visit, and enforced that attention to bodily symptoms which Miss Brontë was too apt to neglect, from a fear of becoming nervous herself about her own state, and thus infecting her father. But she could scarcely help feeling much depressed in spirits as the anniversary of her sister Emily's death came round; all the recollections connected with it were painful, yet there were no outward events to call off her attention, and prevent them from pressing hard upon her. At this time, as at many others, I find her alluding in her letters to the solace which she found in the books sent her from Cornhill.
>
> 'What, I sometimes ask, could I do without them? I have recourse to them as to friends; they shorten and cheer many an hour that would be too long and too desolate otherwise; even when my tired sight will not permit me to continue reading, it is pleasant to see them on the shelf, or on the table. I am still very rich, for my stock is far from exhausted. Some other friends have sent me books lately. The perusal

of Harriet Martineau's *Eastern Life* has afforded me great pleasure; and I have found a deep and interesting subject of study in Newman's work on the *Soul*. Have you read this work? It is daring, – it may be mistaken, – but is pure and elevated. Froude's *Nemesis of Faith* I did not like; I thought it morbid; yet in its pages, too, are found sprinklings of truth.'

Brian Keenan

From *An Evil Cradling* (1992)

Brian Keenan, a teacher from Belfast, went to Beirut in 1985. In 1986 fundamentalist Shi'ite militiamen kidnapped him and held him hostage for four and a half years. For much of this time his only contact with the outside world was through his captors and, later, fellow hostages. In his account of the years of captivity he describes the psychological effects of being a prisoner and the friendships he formed with the other men who had been kidnapped.

> Another day. The Shuffling Acolyte [Keenan's nickname for one of the guards] and I take part in our daily ritual, that long short walk to the toilet. That same walk back and I am home again. I don't look any more at the food, knowing its monotony will not change, not even its place on my filthy floor. The door closes, the padlock rattling, and it's over again for another day. With calm, disinterested deliberation I pull from my head the filthy towel that blinds me, and slowly turn to go like a dog well-trained to its corner, to sit again, and wait and wait, forever waiting. I look at this food I know to be the same as it has always been.
>
> But wait. My eyes are almost burned by what I see. There's a bowl in front of me that wasn't there before. A brown button bowl and in it some apricots, some small oranges, some nuts, cherries, a banana. The fruits, the colours, mesmerise me in a quiet rapture that spins through my head. I am entranced by colour. I lift an orange into the flat filthy palm of my hand and feel and smell and lick it. The colour orange, the colour, the colour, my God the colour orange. Before me is a feast of colour. I feel myself begin to dance, slowly, I am intoxicated by colour. I feel the colour in a quiet somnambulant rage. Such wonder, such absolute wonder in such an insignificant fruit.

Doris Lessing

From *Alfred and Emily* (2008)

The first extract from *Alfred and Emily* is taken from the part of the book in which Lessing creates a fictional life for her parents: they marry other people; her mother, Emily, finds fulfilment through good works and her father, Alfred, is not scarred by the First World War because in Lessing's version war is avoided. In the second extract

Lessing uses a description of the contents of her mother's 'Wanted on Voyage' trunk to convey the disappointment Emily felt in the reality of life in Rhodesia.

It was occurring to Daisy that Emily had recently lost a husband, but Daisy had secretly believed her friend would be pleased to get rid of him. William, as a poetical young doctor, had had all the nurses in love with him. But William Martin-White was a different matter, stiff and severe, and people were afraid of him. She was. It did not occur to her that she herself was a pretty formidable figure in the hospital hierarchy.

Daisy enquired, 'Are you thinking of marrying again, Emily?'

'God, no,' said Emily, forcefully.

This confirmed what Daisy had thought and now she said, 'Put out your candle. I want to tell you something.'

Emily obeyed. It was a little blue enamel candlestick, and the candle was a stump. She loved the pretty candlestick, and often left the candle burning, as a sort of company.

'Now, Emily,' said Daisy, lying down, but leaving her candle burning enough to see if Emily had become herself again, 'I haven't told you this, I am pretty sure, I've been running around and around, because of Rupert. He wants a wedding soon... But, you see, he is involved with a society for the children of the East End. I am sure you know this, but there is such dreadful poverty there.'

Emily had not for years been conscious of much poverty. The people who had come to her parties were all well-off, if not rich. When she came to think of it, servants were the closest she had come to London poverty. Here, in the weeks she had been with the Lanes, she had visited the Redways in their fine house and had not been in the cottages of the farm workers. Their children, she thought, were not lacking in anything. They were warmly dressed and had plenty to eat. She believed their schools weren't up to much, though.

Britain was wealthy, was booming, was at a level of prosperity the leader writers and public figures congratulated themselves and everybody on. Britain had not had a war since the Boer War; nor were there wars in Western Europe, which was on a high level of well-being. It was enough only to contrast the dreadful situation of the old Austrian Empire and the Turkish Empire, in collapse, to know that keeping out of war was a recipe for prosperity.

Various skirmishes in Africa, which could have grown worse, were damped down, because 'Why spoil what we have?' France, Germany, the Low Countries were booming.

But the riches of Britain, which was as full of big houses and high-living people as it had been in Edwardian times, did not seem to percolate downwards.

Daisy, keeping an eye on Emily in case she would start her crying again, sat up, and told her that the children of the East End ('and I'm only talking about London, mind you') were as pitifully ill-fed, unclad, dirty 'as a lot of little savages, Emily. Anyway, Rupert is going to set up this society, and we have a good many well-known supporters. We aim to change the East End. It is a disgrace that a great rich city like London should tolerate such poverty.' She went on for a while, saw that Emily had gone to sleep, and went to sleep herself.

****

But then, one day, just like that, she said yes; some new disappointment must have overtaken her, telling her that, no, she would never wear those frocks, those feathery boas, the brocade shoes, the satin evening cloaks, whose hems were weighed with deep strips of diamante or embroidery.

The middle part of the trunk held the frocks, and as we opened it, moths flew up.

'I should have put in more mothballs,' remarked my mother, as dry as you like, almost indifferent, just as if she was not about to see her precious dreams for the frocks disappear into moth holes. She sat there, my mother, while my avid grubby clumsy hands took off layers of crisp white paper – well, not so crisp now. I laid on the floor a sage green lace dress, with long sleeves and, in the front, covering a deep V, a wisp of the palest pink chiffon, or some scrap of flesh-coloured stuff. 'A dinner dress,' murmured my mother. 'I never actually wore it. It was too formal for the voyage.' A dinner dress! People wore clothes especially made to eat their dinner in? 'It's for a dinner party, you see,' she remarked, in that offhand voice, dry from keeping the tears at bay.

There it lay, on the floor, the tissue paper in rolls and puffs around it.

It was mid-calf, 1924. Since then skirts had climbed to the knee and were low again, on the dresses that were winsome and girlish and feminine. I took out a slithery mass, which, laid on top of the sage dinner dress, then lifted up to see, consisted of two sheets of midnight blue sequins, back and front, on a backing of dark blue chiffon.

'I wore that,' murmured my mother, 'on the last night of the voyage at the captain's table. People noticed it'.

I held it up. It was heavy. 'Just look at those gorgeous sequins.' Tiny holes appeared in the chiffon. The sequins dragged in places because the moth had got at the material they were stitched on.

That was a dress to admire, not to love.

The next was a dark blue confection, with a plain round-necked top, falling from the hips in layers of tulle, or chiffon, or something like that. The moths had had a real go at those skirts.

'That's a ball dress,' she remarked, 'but since I bought it, there hasn't been a ball.'

Then came a black lace dress, the skirt again falling from the hips, over an emerald green lip. There were lace sleeves to just above the elbow.

The idea would be, said my mother, instructing me, to wear a bracelet under the lace on one arm.

'I see,' I said.

And then *the frock*, the beauty of them all, held up by me so that she could see it. It had the palest grey top, of chiffon, and on the chiffon were traceries of crystal beads. The lowest part, from the hips, was of slightly darker grey, like water rather than mist, and the crystalline tracery on that was a little heavier. The top had wide straps, made of the material with crystals on it folded over. There was a wisp of a little jacket, designed to show the patterns of beads.

'Oh, oh,' I moaned, 'just look, oh, just look.'

And she did just look, and saw … 'I've never worn it,' she said. 'When I saw it hanging there I knew it was my dress. I had to have it, I paid much too much …' and she put out her hand, a fine, elegant hand, worn with farm work, and stroked it.

It was full of moth holes.

There was another dress, of fine green linen. Like the others it flared from the hips to a hemline marked by a deep band of white embroidery. The neckline and the sleeves had the embroidery too.

But when and where would one wear it?

'Imagine,' said my mother, dry as the dust that hung in the air, 'what people would say if I put that on in Banket.'

'But what is it for?'

'That's a garden-party dress.'

A garden party!

'You know the park in Salisbury? Well, imagine it with English trees, and English shrubs and flowers. There would be music, you see, and a big marquee with tea and refreshments.'

And now she was crying, and wiping her eyes.

A dress in georgette – something delicate.

'Look, autumn colours,' said my mother, 'just like a beech wood in autumn.'

The skirt was to mid-calf, in 'handkerchief' points, each one defined by a brown bead.

'I suppose I could wear that here – if there was a party. No, not really.

'I'm being very silly,' she announced, and swept herself up to her feet. 'You'd better have these,' she said. 'You can use them for dressing up. Or cut them up, if you feel like ... I don't care ...' and she ran out of the room to find a place to cry, I suppose.

A dress in silver lamé: the material was silver threads and black woven together. It was going black in patches. It smelled deathly. It had black jet beads around the neck and armholes. They were falling off. They lay scattered about over the other dresses, the floor, like tiny black ants.

And so those lovely frocks did get cut up, and when I was older with a few more inches grown, I tried to put what was left of them on.

But they were not what I wanted to wear, for nineteen-twenties fashions were being mocked, jeered at, ridiculous. It was not till the sixties and the mini-skirt that anyone had a good word to say for those low-waisted frocks.

When I wore one wrapped around my twelve-year-old, thirteen-year-old person, or saw the dog wearing the grey chiffon with crystal beads, which I and my brother put on him, as a joke, my mother looked hard and saw me, dressed in the uniform of an English girls' school, because 'getting-off-the-farm' had more potency with every year that passed and was further away.

Primo Levi

From *If This is a Man* (1947)
Here Levi describes the fight for survival in Auschwitz and his struggle to find words to convey the ordeal.

We fought with all our strength to prevent the arrival of winter. We clung to all the warm hours, at every dusk we tried to keep the sun in the sky for a little longer, but it was all in vain. Yesterday evening the sun went down irrevocably behind a confusion of dirty clouds, chimney stacks and wires, and today it is winter.

We know what it means because we were here last winter; and the others will soon learn. It means that in the course of these months, from October till April, seven out of ten of us will die. Whoever does not die will suffer minute by minute, all day, every day: from the morning before dawn until the distribution of the evening soup we will have to keep our muscles continually tensed, dance from foot to foot, beat our arms under our shoulders against the cold. We will have to spend bread to acquire gloves, and lose hours of sleep to repair them when they become unstitched. As it will no longer be possible to eat in the open, we will have to eat our meals in the hut, on our feet, everyone will be assigned an area of floor as large as a hand, as it is forbidden to rest against the bunks. Wounds will open on everyone's hands, and to be given a bandage will mean waiting every evening for hours on one's feet in the snow and wind.

Just as our hunger is not that feeling of missing a meal, so our way of being cold has need of a new word. We say 'hunger', we say 'tiredness', 'fear', 'pain', we say 'winter' and they are different things. They are free words, created and used by free men who lived in comfort and suffering in their homes. If the Lagers had lasted longer a new, harsh language would have been born; and only this language could express what it means to toil the whole day in the wind, with the temperature below freezing, wearing only a shirt, underpants, cloth jacket and trousers, and in one's body nothing but weakness, hunger and knowledge of the end drawing nearer.

Alison Light

From *Mrs Woolf and the Servants* (2007)

Alison Light uses the hidden lives of Virginia Woolf's servants, such as her cook Nellie Boxall with whom she lived for eighteen years, to contrast the views Woolf held in public with the often conflicting feelings which she expressed in her diaries and letters to friends such as Vita Sackville-West and her sister, Vanessa Bell. Bell's comments about Grace Germany, nurse to her daughter, Angelica, are taken from *Selected Letters of Vanessa Bell*, ed. Regina Marler (1993).

Virginia saw herself as passive in the face of 'the system'; Nellie was 'uneducated', trying to 'let herself in' to a world to which she did not belong. But education was not simply a matter of learning or schooling. Virginia was herself ambivalent about the formal education which she had missed, sometimes attacking the inequalities which had led to her remaining at home while her male peers attended public school and university, at other times deeply scathing about 'schoolmastering', the narrowness of university dons (especially those who taught English literature), and the competitive, prize-winning mentality which struck her as ludicrous and demeaning. She saw it as profoundly masculine, and both *A Room of One's Own* and *Three Guineas* hope that women might create a different model of education. As more people were becoming literate, there were debates across the political spectrum as to what might constitute a vibrant education for the working classes, one which would go beyond the rote-learning and exam-passing which merely pushed people into jobs. Yet when Virginia called herself 'uneducated', as she often did, she was playing down the advantages that growing up in a bookish, articulate home had conferred on her, the cultural confidence or cultural capital she had inherited – and which other people so clearly lacked. 'Culture' was by definition unavailable to *arrivistes*, foreigners – especially Americans – and the lower orders; most of the middle class were also philistine as were the aristocrats (Vita Sackville-West, for instance, had a perfect body but was a 'donkey' when it came to brains). Vanessa put it frankly: alone in Cassis with Angelica and Grace, it seemed silly not to eat together but she missed 'grown-up educated companions'. Grace was 'extraordinarily nice', Vanessa wrote to Virginia, but

> she is, like all the uneducated, completely empty-headed really, and after a bit gets terribly on one's nerves. She either asks me questions, which it is obvious she could answer as well as I can, or she tells me things she has already told me dozens of times about the Harlands [Keynes's servants]. One has practically no common ground in common. I am rather interested to see what does happen with the lower classes, as Grace is a very good specimen, not only unusually nice, but more ready than most to try to understand other things, reading all she can get hold of and making desperate efforts towards culture.

Nonetheless Grace's 'desperate efforts' were doomed. Vanessa added, 'there's something I suppose in having educated grandparents, for already Angelica [aged eight] is capable of understanding things in a way one can see Grace never will'. Vanessa looked forward to ending her 'inquiries into the lower class mind' when Duncan Grant arrived and Grace was 'relegated' to the kitchen again. Meanwhile Virginia's solution to Nellie's encroachment on her territory was to opt for a 'complete renovation of domestic life'. She would write her orders for dinner in a book, 'thus putting a glass between' herself and Nellie. It's hard to see how this would help.

Janet Malcolm

From *The Silent Woman* (1994)

In this first extract, which is taken from close to the start of *The Silent Woman*, Janet Malcolm muses on the nature of biography. In the second extract she describes her meeting with Ted Hughes's sister, Olwyn, who has kept a fiercely protective eye over the Hughes estate and legacy.

> Biography is the medium through which the remaining secrets of the famous dead are taken from them and dumped out in full view of the world. The biographer at work, indeed, is like the professional burglar, breaking into a house, rifling through certain drawers that he has good reason to think contain the jewelry and money, and triumphantly bearing his loot away. The voyeurism and busybodyism

that impel writers and readers of biography alike are obscured by an apparatus of scholarship designed to give the enterprise an appearance of banklike blandness and solidity. The biographer is portrayed almost as a kind of benefactor. He is seen as sacrificing years of his life to his task, tirelessly sitting in archives and libraries and patiently conducting interviews with witnesses. There is no length he will not go to, and the more his book reflects his industry the more the reader believes that he is having an elevating literary experience, rather than simply listening to backstairs gossip and reading other people's mail. The transgressive nature of biography is rarely acknowledged, but it is the only explanation for biography's status as a popular genre. The reader's amazing tolerance (which he would extend to no novel written half as badly as most biographies) makes sense only when seen as a kind of collusion between him and the biographer in an excitingly forbidden undertaking: tiptoeing down the corridor together, to stand in front of the bedroom door and try to peep through the keyhole.

Every now and then, a biography comes along that strangely displeases the public. Something causes the reader to back away from the writer and refuse to accompany him down the corridor. What the reader has usually heard in the text – what has alerted him to danger – is the sound of doubt, the sound of a crack opening in the wall of the biographer's self-assurance. As a burglar should not pause to discuss with his accomplice the rights and wrongs of burglary while he is jimmying a lock, so a biographer ought not to introduce doubts about the legitimacy of the biographical enterprise. The biography-loving public does not want to hear that biography is a flawed genre. It prefers to believe that certain biographers are bad guys.

****

On February 11, 1991, I sat eating lunch with Olwyn Hughes in an almost empty Indian restaurant in London's Camden Town. London itself had a hushed, emptied-out feeling. The Gulf War had begun a few weeks earlier; terrorism was feared, and travel had halted – my hotel was three-quarters empty. The weather was contributing to the city's mutedness. A spell of snow and freezing weather, for which the nation was unprepared, had set in, a siege of cold like the one that England was undergoing at the time of Plath's death, which Alvarez unforgettably rendered in his memoir:

> The snow began just after Christmas and would not let up. By New Year the whole country had ground to a halt. The trains froze on the tracks, the abandoned trucks froze on the roads. The power stations, overloaded by million upon pathetic million of hopeless

electric fires, broke down continually; not that the fires mattered, since the electricians were mostly out on strike. Water pipes froze solid; for a bath you had to scheme and cajole those rare friends with centrally heated houses, who became rarer and less friendly as the weeks dragged on. Doing the dishes became a major operation. The gastric rumble of water in outdated plumbing was sweeter than the sound of mandolins. Weight for weight, plumbers were as expensive as smoked salmon and harder to find. The gas failed and Sunday roasts were raw. The lights failed and candles, of course, were unobtainable. Nerves failed and marriages crumbled. Finally, the heart failed. It seemed the cold would never end. Nag, nag, nag.

Now, twenty-eight years later, the English were still stubbornly clinging to their notion that severe winter weather comes so infrequently to their green and pleasant land that preparing for it is not worthwhile, and I was thus able to experience at first hand some of Plath's frustration and feeling of stuckness during the winter of her suicide. I had sat for hours in an unheated train – grounded at a local station because the doors had frozen shut – and observed my fellow passengers, who sat docile and expressionless, incurious about their fate, in a kind of exaltation of uncomplaining discomfort. I had walked through the city covered with treacherous hard-frozen snow and recalled Plath's 'humorous' essay 'Snow Blitz,' written shortly before her death, in which her American impatience with English passivity and its attendant moral superiority kept breaking through the surface tone of amused detachment.

'Sylvia died this month,' I said to Olwyn in the Indian restaurant. 'On which day was it?'

'It happens to be today,' she said. 'I realised it yesterday, when I was dating a letter to you. It's strange.'

'The house on Fitzroy Road where she died is near here, isn't it?' I said. 'After lunch, would you walk over there with me?'

'Darling, I don't think I want to do that,' Olwyn said. She lit a cigarette, and as I looked at her through the smoke I recalled an entry in *Letters Home*, dated November 21, 1956, which gives Plath's first impression of her new sister-in-law:

Olwyn, Ted's sister, stopped by this weekend on her way from a stay at home to her job in Paris. She is 28 and very startlingly beautiful with amber-gold hair and eyes. I cooked a big roast beef dinner, with red wine and strawberries and cream. She reminds me of a changeling, somehow, who will never get old. She is, however, quite selfish and squanders money on herself continually in extravagances of clothes and cigarettes, while she still owes Ted 50 pounds. But in spite of this, I do like her.

Plath's sense of Olwyn as a fey creature who would never grow old was brilliantly prescient. Although Olwyn today 'looks her age' – isn't one of those astonishingly young-looking older women the modern world is full of – neither does she look like the usual woman in her sixties. There is something of the schoolgirl about her, an atmosphere of daring and disobedience, a hint of bohemianism. The hair is still amber-gold; the face is handsome and cared for. At the same time, there is something forbidding and imposing about her. Like Hughes (and Plath), she is large-boned and tall, and as she sat in the restaurant with her coat over her shoulders, in a hunched posture that unsettlingly fused wilfulness and dejection, I thought of Dürer's allegorical rendering of Melancholy. In person, as in her letters, Olwyn is magnificently indifferent to the question of what her interlocutor does or doesn't know about the outrages that writers about Plath have committed or will commit. She simply pours out anger at and contempt for the people she has had to deal with in her position as literary agent to the Plath estate. She is like the principal of a school or the warden of a prison: students or inmates come and go, while she remains. A rowdy new class of freshmen was about to arrive. Ronald Hayman and Paul Alexander were soon to publish their defiantly unauthorized biographies, and Jacqueline Rose was about to come out with a literary study that would impertinently challenge the editing of *The Journals* and *Letters Home*. But Olwyn had by no means forgotten the misdemeanors of the alumni, or those of the recently matriculated Anne Stevenson. I had only to touch the sore spot to send her into an aria of derision whose first notes I had heard a few months earlier, and which I would continue to hear throughout our acquaintance. 'Let's face it, Anne was a mistake,' she had said at our first meeting. 'I regret I didn't get somebody brighter, somebody like Hilary Spurling. Sylvia was an intellectual – Anne is not. I had to nanny her along. She wasted a year of my life.' And (in a later recital): 'Anne is a good little poet. She's a little literary lady. She did some good things; there are one or two chapters that are quite nice. She's a passionate little writer. But she doesn't have a lively hungry mind. I hadn't realised that. I was misled by her sober demeanor and her nice tweeds and the fact that she taught. She never quite grasped Sylvia's nature. She got her wrong. She was always imagining she was this sweet emotional girl. But she wasn't.' Now, in the Indian restaurant, Olwyn returned to the theme. 'Anne left all the interesting things out and put the dull things in,' she said. 'She had to put her stamp on everything. She kept one dancing about with her silly little notes. I was exasperated by this rubbish. I wanted the facts to be on record. I didn't know she would write her little personal musings on Sylvia Plath. Biography isn't a poem, it isn't a novel, it's a document.'

| WRITING LIVES

Sylvia Plath

'Morning Song'

This is the first poem in *Ariel* (1965). Unlike much of Plath's work, which addresses her own experience of mental anguish or loss, it describes the joy of becoming a mother.

Love set you going like a fat gold watch.
The midwife slapped your footsoles, and your bald cry
Took its place among the elements.

Our voices echo, magnifying your arrival. New statue.
In a drafty museum, your nakedness
Shadows our safety. We stand round blankly as walls.

I'm no more your mother
Than the cloud that distils a mirror to reflect its own slow
Effacement at the wind's hand.

All night your moth-breath
Flickers among the flat pink roses. I wake to listen:
A far sea moves in my ear.

One cry, and I stumble from bed, cow-heavy and floral
In my Victorian nightgown.
Your mouth opens clean as a cat's. The window square

Whitens and swallows its dull stars. And now you try
Your handful of notes;
The clear vowels rise like balloons.

Plutarch

From *The Lives of the Noble Grecians and Romans*

In this extract from John Dryden's translation, Plutarch compares the Roman politician Brutus (*c*. BC 85–42), and Dion (*c*. BC 408–354), the brother-in-law of Dionysius the Elder, who ruled as tyrant over Syracuse in Sicily.

The greatest thing charged on Brutus is, that he, being saved by Caesar's kindness, having saved all the friends whom he chose to ask for, he moreover accounted a friend, and preferred above many, did yet lay violent hands upon his preserver. Nothing like this could be objected against Dion; quite the contrary; whilst he was of Dionysius's family and his friend, he did good service and was useful to him; but driven from his country, wronged in his wife, and his estate lost, he openly entered upon a war just and lawful.

Does not, however, the matter turn the other way? For the chief glory of both was their hatred of tyranny, and abhorrence of wickedness. This was unmixed and sincere in Brutus; for he had no private quarrel with Caesar, but went into the risk singly for the liberty of his country. The other, had he not been privately injured, had not fought. This is plain from Plato's epistles, where it is shown that he was turned out, and did not forsake the court to wage war upon Dionysius. Moreover, the public good made Brutus Pompey's friend (instead of his enemy as he had been) and Caesar's enemy; since he proposed for his hatred and his friendship no other end and standard but justice. Dion was very serviceable to Dionysius whilst in favour; when no longer trusted, he grew angry and fell to arms. And, for this reason, not even were his own friends all of them satisfied with his undertaking, or quite assured that, having overcome Dionysius, he might not settle the government on himself, deceiving his fellow-citizens by some less obnoxious name than tyranny. But the very enemies of Brutus would say that he had no other end or aim, from first to last, save only to restore to the Roman people their ancient government.

James Shapiro

From *1599, A Year in the Life of William Shakespeare* (2005)

Shapiro shows how a sermon by one of the country's most famous preachers, Lancelot Andrewes, may have influenced Shakespeare when he was writing *Henry the Fifth*. Andrewes uses the sermon to sanction the Earl of Essex's plans to punish the Earl of Tyrone for the rebellion he was leading in Ireland.

When scholars talk about the sources of Shakespeare's plays, they almost always mean printed books like Holinshed's *Chronicles* that they themselves can read; but Shakespeare's was an aural culture, the music of which has long faded. Lost to us are the unrecorded sounds reverberating around him – street cries of vendors, church bells, regional and foreign accents, scraps of overheard conversation, and countless bits of speech and noise that filled the densely packed capital. Some of these made their way into Shakespeare's writing, others impeded it, and still others were a kind of precondition for it. In a culture where so little was written down, memories had to be strong. Only a tiny percentage of Elizabethan sermons were committed to print, so it's a stroke of luck that Andrewes's war sermon was one of them, for the evidence suggests that elements of it inspired (or uncannily parallelled) the play that Shakespeare was now completing.

Andrewes began his sermon in the usual fashion by quoting the Scripture upon which he would elaborate – 'When thou goest out, with the host against thine enemies, keep thee then from all wickedness'

– before launching into a dramatic start that underscored just how directly the Bible spoke to the current military crisis in Ireland. 'To entitle this time to this text, or to show it pertinent to the present occasion, will ask no long preface. "When thou goest forth, etc." This when is now. There be enemies; and we have an host: It is going forth.' It's worth quoting at length (like Shakespeare's prose, it's best read aloud) to catch Andrewes's distinctive voice – abrupt, jagged, full of emphases, crammed with witty conceits and word-play – a style beloved of the Elizabethans: 'This our host so going forth, our hearts desire and prayer unto God is, that they may happily go, and thrice happily come again; with joy and triumph, to her sacred Majesty; honour to themselves; and general contentment to the whole land.' Note the thumping reiteration of 'this time' and 'this day':

> These former years, this time of the fast, and this day, the first day of it (both) ministered an occasion to call from an abstinence from sin. This day, and this time being set out by the Church's appointment to that end. Now, besides that ordinary, of other years, God, this year, hath sent us another, this time of war, and that, a very seasonable time too, wherein to repent and retire from sins … This is the sum … that our giving over sin might procure the good speed to our going forth; even an honourable and happy return.

Just five weeks later London audiences would hear far more rousing sentiments in a similar celebration of troops going into battle 'this day' in *Henry the Fifth*:

> This day is called the Feast of Crispian.
> He that outlives this day and comes safe home
> Will stand a-tiptoe when this day is named
> And rouse him at the name of Crispian.
> He that shall see this day and live old age
> Will yearly on the vigil feast his neighbours
> And say, 'Tomorrow is Saint Crispian.'
> Then will he strip his sleeve and show his scars,
> And say, 'These wounds I had on Crispin's Day.'
> (IV, iii, 40–48)

The thrust of Andrewes's speech is to sanction, if not bless, the plan to crush Tyrone, who has broken faith: 'Here, here have been diverse princely favours vouchsafed, and most unkindly rejected; means of clemency many times most graciously offered, and most ungraciously refused; yea, faith falsified, and expectation deluded; contempt upon contempt heaped up, that the measure is full. These then are the enemies against, and this the time when.' Though offering unconditional support for the campaign, Andrewes doesn't shy away from chiding the government for its past habit of sending over ill-equipped soldiers. This time must be different: 'Victuals must be supplied ... Pay must be thought of ... We must "go forth with our host"... "with our host", not a heap of naked or starved men.' And perhaps turning directly to Essex (who had recently boasted that he 'would have thought danger a sport and death a feast'), Andrewes warns: 'War is no matter of sport.' It 'may be "sport" in the beginning; it will be "bitterness in the end", if it hold long.' It was a sermon sure to meet with his monarch's approval.

There are a number of moments in *Henry the Fifth* that owe nothing to either the chronicles or to Shakespeare's dramatic sources. They are related to the two strands of Andrewes's argument in this sermon: the theological justification for an aggressive offensive war and the need for those who go off to war to purge themselves of sin. *Henry the Fifth* opens with English clergymen debating an imminent military campaign, followed not long after by one of the longest speeches in any of Shakespeare's plays, a virtual sermon by the Archbishop of Canterbury insisting on the legitimacy of Henry's offensive war against his neighbouring country. Even as Andrewes assures Elizabeth, Essex and the rest of the court that the war is 'no sin, but lawful' and that 'not only defensive war, but offensive war too hath his "when"', Canterbury argues in Shakespeare's play that Henry's cause is lawful, just, and has the clergy's blessing.

The connection between Andrewes's sermon and Shakespeare's play extends to the scene in which the disguised Henry V argues with his troops on the eve of the battle of Agincourt. At the climax of this scene the King refuses to accept his soldiers' argument that if the war is unjust, their guilt is upon his head. When Henry insists rather that 'every subject's soul is his own' and that every soldier should 'wash every mote out of his conscience', he might as well be paraphrasing Andrewes's contention that the act of going to war demands a collective renunciation of sin: 'What a thing this is, how great, gross and foul and incongruity it is, to pour ourselves into sin at the very time when we go forth to correct sin: To set forth to punish rebels when we ourselves are in rebellion against God?' Finally, Andrewes's belief that the victory belongs to God not man – 'that the safe and speedy coming again of them that "now go forth"... dependeth upon God's "going forth with them"' – is echoed in the play by Henry's assertion that the victory is God's alone:

O God, thy arm was here!
And not to us, but to thy arm alone,
Ascribe we all.

(IV, viii, 106-8)

With Andrewes's cadences ringing in his ears, Shakespeare returned to London that day to sign off on the Globe contract. The break for Lent left him a few precious weeks to finish the play before he had to turn it over, first to the Master of the Revels for approval and then to the actors to learn their lines in time for the reopening of the theatres in late March.

Zadie Smith and Ian McEwan

From interview in *Believer Book of Writers Talking to Writers* (2005)

Zadie Smith (ZS) interviewed Ian McEwan (IM) in his home in central London in Spring 2005 to discuss his writing. The interview took place in the year that his novel, *Saturday*, was published. The book's central character, a neurosurgeon called Dr Henry Perowne, lives in a house identical to McEwan's.

ZS: There is a lot in *Saturday* of the details of your own existence.

IM: It is the first time I've really cannibalised my life.

ZS: It is the first time. And I wondered what happens next?

IM: Next, I will almost certainly have an entirely invented set of circumstances.

ZS: There's always a difference, though. Certainly I find the more I carry on at this lark the less I have time for imagined, physical detail. I just don't do it. If I need a sofa, I look across the room and there's a sofa. If I need a lamppost, there's a lamppost in the street. I can't conjure lampposts out of nothing. Maybe when I was fourteen. That's completely beyond me now.

IM: No, quite. And also how much furniture does one need any more? In answer to your question, having cannibalised my life for this novel, it makes the next one easier. I'm left with everything that's not *this* [points around the room], and that's a hell of a lot. I have no idea what it will be. There's also all the past which I've never really borrowed – my childhood. But I don't know. Naturally when people say 'You've got better' I get a bit pissed off and say 'Well, what was wrong with the others? What was I doing wrong before?'

ZS: Well, it's not that the earlier stuff was worse, but it's that the tools and machinery of this one work so very smoothly, one feels completely confident as a reader. You've no problem at all anymore with 'making a novel'. When I think of both my novels the second halves of both are rubbish because of basic, technical inability. When you're younger every page is still a struggle. And when I read *Saturday* I just felt: well, 'making a novel' is the least of your bloody problems, mate. Same with Roth. There are other things that are being developed – ideas, themes, larger ambitions to do with a canon of work – but the 'making a novel' bit feels like it's done effortlessly. Maybe that's not how it is at all. But I wondered whether the autobiographical stuff makes the composition process a slightly smoother process.

IM: I have to say I thought it would be. I made this decision, OK, I will blatantly use my life in this next novel so that will save me an awful lot of time. Actually it didn't. It was just as much a struggle. Even when I was actually using the internal layout of this house for the scenes, it rarely occurred to me as I walked about this house that this was the same house in the book. It's somehow a map of a parallel house.

ZS: Talking of parallels, there's a paragraph in *Saturday* about surgery, apparently, but it seems to me to be about writing.

IM: Oh, well done.

ZS: I read it and thought it can't be about anything else. You know the paragraph I mean? 'For the past two hours he's been in a dream of absorption' – it's such an exact description of what it's like to write when it's going well. And my favourite line is when you talk about him feeling 'calm and spacious, fully qualified to exist. It's a feeling of clarified emptiness, of deep, muted joy.' The events you put next to it, as comparative experiences – the love-making and listening to Theo's song – are two human states which are often advertised as bringing similar pleasure; basically, personal relations and art. But the book seems to suggest that there is a deeper happiness that one can only find in work, or at least, creative work. And I felt that joy coming off the book in every direction. Joy at being a writer!

IM: I'm glad that you found that paragraph. I knew I wanted to write a major operation at the end but it would really be about writing, about making art. So it starts with him picking up a paintbrush. Or rather, I was *so* sure, when I went for the operation, that Neil Pritchard the surgeon, when he paints the marks on the patient, was using a two-inch paintbrush. And when I sent him the last draft, just to check it one last time he said, 'I don't use a paintbrush,' and I said, 'But surely surgeons do,' and he said, 'No, no. I was so disappointed personally. He dips the paintbrush in yellow paint and as the Aria of the Goldberg Variations starts, he makes his first stroke and it is a moment of artistic engagement … But very, very reluctantly I had to replace it with a sponge on a flap.

ZS: The joy of the extended analogy is that it allows you to write about writing as work. Usually when you read books about being a novelist, all you really get is the character at lunches and his publishing routines, and that's nothing to do with the process of writing. It's so hard to sit down and write about that procedure, but I feel that metaphorically it's done here.

IM: The dream, surely, Zadie, that we all have, is to write this beautiful paragraph that actually is describing something but at the same time in another voice is writing a commentary on its own creation, without having to be a story about a writer.

Virginia Woolf

From *The Diary of Virginia Woolf, volume III, 1925–30*

These two extracts from Virginia Woolf's diary in 1927 – 14 March and 20 September – provide an insight into how books and ideas formed and changed in her mind.

Monday 14 March 1927

Although annoyed that I have not heard from Vita by this post nor yet last week, annoyed sentimentally, & partly from vanity – still I must record the conception last night between 12 & one of a new book. I said I would be on the watch for symptoms of this extremely mysterious process. For some weeks, since finishing *The Lighthouse* I have thought myself virgin, passive, blank of ideas. I toyed vaguely with some thoughts of a flower whose petals fall; of time all telescoped into one lucid channel through wh. my heroine was to pass at will. The petals falling. But nothing came of it. I shirked the effort – seemed to have no impulse that way, supposed that I had worked out my vein. Faith Henderson came to tea, &, valiantly beating the waters of conversation, I sketched the possibilities which an unattractive woman, penniless, alone, might yet bring into being. I began imagining the position – how she would stop a motor on the Dover road, & so get to Dover: cross the channel: &c. It struck me, vaguely, that I might write a Defoe narrative for fun. Suddenly between twelve & one I conceived a whole fantasy to be called 'The Jessamy Brides' – why, I wonder? I have rayed round it several scenes. Two women, poor, solitary at the top of a house. One can see anything (for this is all fantasy) the Tower Bridge, clouds, aeroplanes. Also old men listening in the room over the way. Everything is to be tumbled in pall mall. It is to be written as I write letters at the top of my speed: on the ladies of Llangollen; on Mrs Fladgate; on people passing. No attempt is to be made to realise the character. Sapphism is to be suggested. Satire is to be the main note – satire & wildness. The Ladies are to have Constantinople in view. Dreams of golden domes. My own lyric vein is to be satirised. Everything mocked. And it is to end with three dots ... so. For the truth is I feel the need of an escapade after these serious poetic experimental books whose form is always so closely considered. I want to kick up my heels & be off. I want to embody all those innumerable little ideas & tiny stories which flash into my mind at all seasons. I think this will be great fun to write; & it will rest my head before starting the very serious, mystical poetical work which I want to come next. Meanwhile, before I can touch the Jessamy Brides, I have to write my book on fiction & that wont be done till January, I suppose. I might dash off a page or two now & then by way of experiment. And it is possible that the idea will evaporate. Anyhow this records the odd hurried unexpected way in which these things suddenly create themselves – one thing on top of another in about an hour. So I made up *Jacob's Room* looking at the fire at Hogarth House; so I made up *The Lighthouse* one afternoon in the square here.

****

Tuesday 20 September 1927
One of these days, though, I shall sketch here, like a grand historical picture, the outlines of all my friends. I was thinking of this in bed last night, & for some reason I thought I would begin with a sketch of Gerald Brennan. There may be something in this idea. It might be a way of writing the memoirs of one's own times during people's lifetimes. It might be a most amusing book. The question is how to do it. Vita should be Orlando, a young nobleman. There should be Lytton. & it should be truthful; but fantastic. Roger. Duncan. Clive. Adrian. Their lives should be related. But I can think of more books than I shall ever be able to write. How many little stories come into my head! For instance: Ethel Sands not looking at her letters. What this implies. One might write a book of short significant separate scenes. She did not open her letters.

   We motored to Long Barn & back yesterday, through suburbs for the most part. All Hampstead, red, sanitary, earnest, view gazing, breeze requiring is lodged in the heights of Ashdown Forest. Now & again one comes on something consciously preserved like the Wren house at Groombridge. One stops the motor & looks. So do other motorists. We found Vita & Dotty sitting over a log fire. Dottie is going to spend £200 a year on poetry: to edit a series of books of unsaleable poetry. This £200 she was giving to the Poetry Bookshop, but deterred by his earnestness & his drunkenness she is crying off: & has laid it at our feet. There will be much comment she says at this. People will say she is buying her way into Bloomsbury. The children were there; Nigel very shabby: Vita dressed him as a Russian boy 'Don't. It makes me look like a little girl,' he said. There was the French tutor who never spoke. Dotty Byronic in her dress, but much improved over the London Dotty. They do not yet know what is to become of Harold, who has refused to go to Buda Pesth.

Critical approaches

- How has Doris Lessing written about her life?

- How have critics responded to her different approaches to life writing?

- Are there any aspects of Lessing's approach to life writing that are particularly daring or experimental?

Part 4 of *Writing Lives* focuses on the autobiographical writings of Doris Lessing and in particular, *Alfred and Emily* (2008), in which she explores the lives of her parents using a structure that is part memoir and part fiction. It will examine how Lessing's approach to writing about herself and her family has evolved over a long career, from the autobiographical elements in her early fiction to the two-volume autobiography written when she was in her seventies, and to *Alfred and Emily*, published when she was nearly ninety and had recently won the Nobel Prize for Literature.

Lessing has written over fifty books – many of them containing an element of autobiography – and has addressed issues including racism, radical politics, feminism and the disintegration of the family. Her work includes operas, science fiction, short stories, drama and poetry. She was born in Persia (modern-day Iran) to British parents and grew up in Rhodesia (now Zimbabwe), where her family struggled to make a living from farming. She moved to Britain in 1949 where her first novel, *The Grass is Singing* (1950), was published. Like many of her novels it is set in Africa and explores, among other issues, the relationship between white colonial settlers and the indigenous black people. *Martha Quest* (1952), the first in the *Children of Violence* series, also draws heavily on her childhood in Africa. In *Under My Skin* (1994), the first volume of her autobiography, she addresses the question of the extent to which *Martha Quest* is autobiographical:

> Partly it is, and partly it is not, comes the author's reply, often enough in an irritated voice, because the question seems irrelevant: what she has tried to do is to take the story out of the personal into the general. 'If I had wanted to write autobiography then I would have done it, I wouldn't have written a novel.'

The autobiographical writings of Doris Lessing

Under My Skin tells the story of Lessing's life to 1949, and was written as 'self-defence' against the biographies she knew others were compiling. It won the James Tait Black Memorial Prize for biography and was followed by a second volume, *Walking in the Shade* which continued the account until 1962. A third volume was expected, but Lessing appears to have abandoned this in favour of a less conventional approach to autobiography in *Alfred and Emily*.

In Chapter two of *Under My Skin* she writes:

> Telling the truth or not telling it, and how much, is a lesser problem than the one of shifting perspectives, for you see your life differently at different stages, like climbing a mountain while the landscape changes with every turn in the path. Had I written this when I was thirty, it would have been a pretty combative document. In my forties, a wail of despair and guilt: oh my God, how could I have done this or that? Now I look back at that child, that girl, that young woman, with a more and more detached curiosity. Old people may be observed peering into their pasts, *Why?* – they are asking themselves. *How did that happen?* I try to see my past selves as someone else might, and then put myself back inside one of them, and am at once submerged in a hot struggle of emotion, justified by thoughts and ideas I now judge wrong.

The chapter ends with: 'I am trying to write this book honestly. But were I to write it aged eighty-five, how different would it be?'

Lessing was almost ninety when *Alfred and Emily* appeared. Critics approached the book knowing that she had just won the Nobel Prize and was one of the most respected living authors.

▶ Are there any other ways in which an autobiography or memoir written when the author is elderly might differ from one written in their youth or middle age?

Alfred and Emily

Lessing starts with a foreword that explains the effect the First World War had on her parents, how it 'did them both in'. Her father, Alfred Taylor, lost a leg and never recovered from the horrors he had seen in the trenches; her mother, Emily McVeagh, lost the love of her life – a doctor who drowned in the Channel on his way home from the war. 'That war, the Great War, the war that would end all war, squatted over my childhood …' Lessing writes.

The book is then split in two. The first half takes the form of a novella in which Lessing imagines how her parents' lives might have been if there had been no war. In it she gives her father his 'heart's desire' – the chance to become an English farmer. She is not quite as generous towards her mother, who is not allowed to fulfil her wish of becoming a hospital matron but instead marries a cardiologist. It is only when he dies suddenly that she is allowed to find fulfilment through good works and a talent for storytelling. In this version of their lives, Alfred and Emily end up with other partners and Doris is not born.

'An explanation', in which Lessing tells the reader how she arrived at this fictional version of her parents' lives, immediately follows the end of Part One:

Writing about my father's imagined life, my mother's, I have relied not only on traits of character that may be extrapolated, or extended, but on tones of voice, sighs, wistful looks, signs as slight as those used by skilful trackers.

An extract from an encyclopaedia entry on the Royal Free Hospital, where both the real and the imagined Emily worked, concludes Part One. The second part of the book starts with an extract from *Lady Chatterley's Lover* by D.H. Lawrence:

And dimly she realised one of the great laws of the human soul: that when the emotional soul receives a wounding shock, which does not kill the body, the soul seems to recover as the body recovers. But this is only appearance. It is, really, only the mechanism of re-assumed habit. Slowly, slowly the wound to the soul begins to make itself felt, like a bruise which only slowly deepens its terrible ache, till it fills all the psyche. And when we think we have recovered and forgotten, it is then that the terrible after-effects have to be encountered at their worst.

▶ How effective do you think the above extract from Lawrence, together with the use of an encyclopaedia entry, might be in marking the change from the fictional to the factual sections of the book?

In 'Part Two, Alfred and Emily; Two Lives' Lessing explains what really happened to her parents: how they met when her mother nursed Alfred after the war, their early years in Persia and their lives of struggle in Rhodesia. This part also includes angry asides about the spread of AIDS in Africa, and the gulf between the rich and the underfed:

Probably the most disgusting sight in the world is to watch plates carried out of an American restaurant, still piled with food, and see the garbage bins in the street piled high with uneaten food. As disgusting as seeing the same in England, food that would feed thousands of hungry people. Hungry and dying. They die, they are dying as I write this …

▶ Compare the two extracts from *Alfred and Emily* (Part 3, pages 87–91). In what ways is the style of each different? Are you surprised by which is taken from the novella and which from the memoir? If so, which elements do you find surprising?

Critical responses to *Alfred and Emily*

When *Alfred and Emily* was published in the UK in spring 2008 critics agreed that Lessing had chosen a daring approach in her latest version of autobiography. 'It's a bold experiment – not life writing so much as the righting of lives …' Blake Morrison commented in the *Guardian*.

Does fiction carry more authority than fact, then? It's an argument which Philip Roth has often had with himself (or with his alter ego, Nathan Zuckerman). And Lessing, like Roth, implies there are no easy answers. Her fiction is fluent but fuzzy; her facts are awkward but vivid. Whereas the scene of a summer cricket match [with which the novella opens] might have come from Robert Graves or Siegfried Sassoon, only Lessing could describe with such particularity the Rhodesian farm she knew as a child: the drought-racked cattle, the thatched house with mud walls, the trunk with her mother's dresses in it (so beautiful, yet never worn), the books, the food, the insects, all itemised in loving detail.

Pamela Norris in the *Literary Review* agrees that the structure is 'a clever idea, a way of making reparation for terror, injury and loss, and also of examining character, and the fascinating "what-ifs?" of human destiny'. But Caroline Moore, writing in the *Daily Telegraph,* describes *Alfred and Emily* as 'this extremely strange book'.

Many critics found the second, 'true' part of the book more engaging than the imagined, first half. Philip Hensher, reviewing the book for the *Spectator* magazine, commented: 'If the first half is speculative and disconcertingly dreamlike, the second is like a bomb going off. "I hated my mother," she says. "I can remember that emotion from the start." ' Part Two is

> ... beautifully caught in a series of novelistic images; the trunk full of evening dresses, garden-party dresses, tea gowns which, decades later, Emily's daughter Doris unpacks, every one unworn and wrecked by moths, or the pet cow which Doris raises, like her own talent, until it takes to forcing its way from the veldt into her bedroom, half-grown. It is – an odd, Lessing-like combination – both furious and relaxed, like a recorded rant by a masterly talker.
>
> The second half is worth the price of admission, though the first, speculative half shows some flagging of energy.

▶ Do you think the way these critics praise the 'novelistic' images of the second half of the book reveals their own attitudes to the limits of non-fiction? To what extent do you think non-fiction can be 'novelistic'?

Moore, in the *Telegraph*, writes:

> I fully expected, therefore, to be more gripped by the first, fictional half of *Alfred and Emily* than by the bitty re-hash offered in the second. Yet as a work of fiction in its own right, the novella is oddly ungripping ... Fragmented nuggets of fact, real and invented, are strung together, and none of the characters is strong enough to bind them. Alfred is less interesting than Emily, both come (as in real life) from emotionally broken families ... In the second half of the book,

the writing is as fragmented as the first, but it is vivid, turbulent, fresh with raw emotion, even when replicating earlier material. Clarity and darkness, honesty and wilful obscurity are tumbled together: the work of a writer who knows that the truths of the heart are hideously complicated, sees them with angry dispassion, yet is still enmired in their 'dark pit'.

Maggie Gee, writing in *The Sunday Times*, also finds the second part more powerful than the first:

The style of the first part is conversational and casual, and the narrative at first moves back and forth between the invented and the actual in a slightly dislocating way. Slowly and surely the real world recedes and both writer and reader are drawn into the invented one, but for me this section could not match the raw power and conviction of the second part.

▶ Both reviewers (above) use the word 'raw' to describe the writing in the second part of the book. What do you think they mean by this?

Paul Binding, writing in *The Times Literary Supplement*, compares Lessing to D.H. Lawrence in the 'unflagging creativity of her verbal harnessing of nature' and singles out her description of the young Lessing's affection for a bull-calf. Binding concludes that the epigraph from *Lady Chatterley's Lover* (see page 107, above) is particularly apposite. Ruth Scurr, in *The Times*, adds that the extract

… resonates with the themes of trauma and repression that run, like fault lines, through her parents' lives, but also reminds us of the immediate context of Lawrence's own novels, his own attempt to take the measure of the First World War.

Scurr feels that the history of the Royal Free Hospital, which concludes Part One, is 'fascinating in its own right' and 'provides a powerful frame for both real and fictional versions of Emily McVeagh's life'.

▶ One reviewer pointed out that Lessing remembers her mother playing the piano to a group of airmen who had just returned from the Second World War and that one of the songs was 'Who do you think you are kidding, Mr Hitler?' Lessing's memory has obviously failed her, the reviewer points out, because this song is not a genuine wartime hit, but was specially composed for the TV sitcom, *Dad's Army*, in the 1960s. Does this factual error – whether unintentional or not – devalue Lessing's account, or does it prove her point that memory is not infallible?

Critical responses to *Alfred and Emily* have ranged from a discussion of the book's bold structure to a debate over which half of the book is more compelling – the novella or the factual version. Doris Lessing was aware of the pitfalls of trying to write about a life when she embarked on the first volume of the autobiography, *Under My Skin*:

> You cannot sit down to write about yourself without **rhetorical questions** of the most tedious kind demanding attention. Our old friend, the Truth, is first. The truth … how much of it to tell, how little? It seems it is agreed this is the first problem of the self-chronicler, and obloquy lies in wait either way …
>
> I have known not a few of the famous, and even one or two of the great, but I do not believe it is the duty of friends, lovers, comrades, to tell all. The older I get the more secrets I have, never to be revealed and this, I know, is a common condition of people my age. And why all this emphasis on kissing and telling? Kisses are the least of it.

Assignments

1   *Alfred and Emily* is divided into two parts. In the first Doris Lessing imagines a different life for her parents in which they marry other people; in the second part she tells the story of what really happened to them. Write an account of how your parents' lives would have been different if they had met other partners and then write about what really happened. Which version did you enjoy writing more and why? How much research did you carry out for each and how did your style differ?

2   How do the character and experiences of Alfred Quest in the novel *Martha Quest* compare with Doris Lessing's own father, Alfred Taylor? In particular, how do the men's experience of the First World War and their visions of the countryside affect their personalities?

3   Read or listen to the acceptance speech that Doris Lessing made when she was awarded the Nobel Prize for Literature (see website in Part 6, page 122). In what ways might future biographers make use of this lecture as a source?

4   Read one of Doris Lessing's novels, for example *Martha Quest* or *The Grass is Singing*, and either *Alfred and Emily* or *Under My Skin*. To what extent is either novel autobiographical in themes and setting? How do you think Lessing's attitude to her mother has affected the way she writes about mother-daughter relationships and about the need for women to be allowed to work?

How to write about life writing

- What is the relationship between the biographer and their subject?

- Is it possible to measure how truthful the writer – whether biographer, author, diarist or letter writer – has been?

- What is the context for the piece of life writing – both the context of when it was written and when it is being read?

The writer and the reader

Writing about a life can take many forms: diaries, letters, memoirs, biography and biographical fiction. Each form has its own conventions and the careful reader can pick up many clues as to its reliability and importance in evaluating a literary life.

When the work was written can be vital. A diary or letter is often more accurate and vivid because it was written at the time of the events that are being described. Much of the power of the diaries of Samuel Pepys (1633–1703), for example, springs from the fact that he was writing about events as they unfurled. On 2 September 1666 he describes the start of what would later be known as the Great Fire of London:

> Some of our mayds sitting up late last night to get things ready against our feast to-day, Jane called us up, about three in the morning, to tell us of a great fire they saw in the City. So I rose and slipped on my nightgowne and went to her window, and thought it to be on the back side of Marke-lane at the farthest; but being unused to such fires ... I thought it far enough off; and so went to bed again and to sleep. About seven rose again ... By and by Jane comes and tells me that she hears that above 300 houses have been burned down ... and that it is now burning down all of Fish-street by London Bridge. So I ... walked to the Tower, and there got up upon one of the high places ... and there did I see houses at that end of the bridge all on fire; and an infinite great fire on this and the other side of the bridge ... So down, with my heart full of trouble, to the Lieutenant of the Tower who tells me that it begun this morning in the King's baker's house in Pudding-lane, and that it hath burned down St Magnus's Church and part of Fish-street already ...

Letters and diaries can offer an insight into the thought processes of an author and provide a direct link between writer and reader. The only possible obstacle might be the way an editor has reproduced the material, but the most faithful editions of letters and diaries will publish the entire work – even to the extent of including original crossings-out and notes in the margin.

A published work may reveal how the author's thinking has changed over time. Doris Lessing's novel, *Martha Quest* (1952), the first volume of her autobiography, *Under My Skin* (1994) and her novella /memoir, *Alfred and Emily* (2008), approach the subject of family and mother-daughter relationships in subtly different ways. J.G. Ballard's accounts of his internment in Shanghai during the Second World War are markedly different in his autobiographical novel, *Empire of the Sun*, which was published when he was fifty-four, and his autobiography, *Miracles of Life*, written when he was in his seventies and suffering from advanced prostate cancer.

The biographer is as significant as their subject. Are they a friend, relative or uncritical admirer? What constraints did they work under? Was the biography authorised, was material withheld or did the subject and their family leave the biographer to draw their own conclusions? Did the biographer start with any preconceptions or theories to prove? What sources have they used and have they allowed the reader to follow these sources in footnotes or other references?

While the biographer may be honest their work may, as Ackroyd has said, become 'a prisoner of its time'. In evaluating a biography the reader should be aware of the historical factors that might influence their approach. Mrs Gaskell sought to redress the balance in favour of Charlotte Brontë; Richard Holmes was preoccupied by the social upheaval of 1960s Europe when he first investigated the lives of the Romantic poets.

In a sense the 'contract' between author and reader has changed. Early letter writers and keepers of journals could not have guessed that their words would be made public; modern authors may be writing in private with an eye to a posthumous public – if their work escapes destruction by jittery relatives. Commercially successful writers today have their thoughts filtered through journalists and public relations machines. Perhaps their publishers' demands for publicity will mean a desire for private reflection and a return to the frank diary entries and exchanges of letters that have provided so much life writing in the past.

Different perspectives: comparing texts

Peter Ackroyd's biography of Charles Dickens and Claire Tomalin's book, *The Invisible Woman*, which explores his secret relationship with the actress Nelly (Ellen) Ternan, both appeared in 1990 and show how two biographers can take completely different approaches to one life.

Dickens and Ternan met in 1857, when he was a forty-five-year-old married man and she was eighteen. The friendship, which may have produced a child, lasted until his death in 1870. Consider this extract in which Tomalin describes how Dickens gave money to unmarried mothers and took an interest in refuges for 'fallen women'.

> This sort of practical work, whatever its origins within his psyche, was greatly to his credit, the response of a decent man to a society that

worked a cruel double standard. The decency appears in his writing here and there, though in a curious form. Dickens spoke up in his journalism for a kinder attitude to erring women and boldly published Mrs Gaskell's story of a Manchester prostitute, 'Lizzie Leigh', in the first issue of *Household Words*; and in his novels he invited compassion rather than censure for women disgraced for sexual reasons, from Nancy in *Oliver Twist* and the smart girl at the race meeting who buys flowers from Little Nell to Lady Dedlock with her guilty secret in *Bleak House*. But his presentation draws entirely on stereotypes of the Fallen Woman. Nancy shows the self-loathing the good reader required of a prostitute; beyond that, she is null. None of the knowledge Dickens picked up from his encounters with such girls and women was ever allowed to get anywhere near his fiction. It's as though an automatic shutter came down when he approached the subject.

- How is your response influenced by your knowledge of the biographer, Claire Tomalin, her reputation and the type of books she writes?

- In what ways is this type of approach typical of a biography written in the late 20th or early 21st century? How would a Victorian biographer have approached Dickens' private life?

- Look carefully at the language that Tomalin uses. In what way do terms such as 'psyche', 'cruel double standard', 'self-loathing' and 'automatic shutter' encourage the reader to look at Dickens' motives from a late 20th century perspective? Why do you think 'Fallen Woman' has capital letters?

- Tomalin appears to have 'taken sides' in favour of Dickens and against the prevailing morals of his time. Is she right to take this approach?

Now compare the extract with the following from Peter Ackroyd's biography, which is three times as long and focuses on Dickens' entire life rather than on his relationship with one person.

> In November he travelled again to France – no doubt once more to see Ellen Ternan, whose presence (it can be surmised) was also casting a shadow over his writings. The danger is of seeing her everywhere, in fact. Can it be Ellen Ternan who stands behind Lizzie Hexam, for example, the 'low born' but gentle heroine of *Our Mutual Friend*? ... Or perhaps we may see the shadow of Ellen Ternan behind the portrait of Bella Wilfer in the same novel ...
> Perhaps. Perhaps not. A writer whose life had been marked by astonishing and abundant invention cannot be presumed to rely upon Ellen Ternan for his portraits of young women. What is certainly true is that in these last two novels, *Great Expectations* and *Our Mutual*

Friend, Dickens has for the first time given serious consideration to the theme of unrequited love. In earlier books it may have been secret or ill-timed, but there was always an equilibrium in which both parties seem to accept that they loved or can be loved; and that, when eventually they declare their love, it is not rejected. But in these last two novels – and in his uncompleted final fiction also – there is torture in love, and despair, and madness. There is some necessary connection between courtship and death in them, too, so that in these last works it is possible to trace the strange curve of Dickens' temperament exploring extremity in art if not necessarily in his life.

▶ Which words or phrases suggest that Ackroyd is making informed guesses about what happened in Dickens' private life and the way in which relationships may have shaped his novels? Do you agree that an author whose life has been marked by 'astonishing and abundant invention' cannot be presumed to rely on one relationship for his 'portraits of young women'?

The context of writing: facts and their emphasis

Ackroyd chose not to emphasise Dickens' relationship with Nelly Ternan; for Tomalin the secret affair became the heart of her biography and a way of re-examining Dickens' attitudes to women and how they appear in his novels. Earlier biographers were unable to delve into this aspect of Dickens' life because the restraints of their time made it impossible for them to tackle such delicate issues and because Dickens' popularity placed him beyond criticism.

While 20th-century biographers were free to explore this element of his life they faced the conundrum of how to interpret comments that were impossible to verify.

Both Ackroyd and Tomalin refer to the testimony of Dickens' daughter, Katey (later Kate Perugini), who asked her friend, Gladys Storey, to place on record certain facts. Storey's book, *Dickens and Daughter*, which was not published until 1939 (ten years after Katey's death), states that Ellen and Dickens had a son who died in infancy. Storey's private papers – which both Ackroyd and Tomalin quote from – refer to a conversation Storey had with Dickens' son, Henry, in which he confirmed his sister's version of events.

In *The Invisible Woman* Tomalin muses over whether to treat Storey's contribution, and other circumstantial evidence, as 'not proven' before continuing her own investigation. In search of the truth she explores a train crash that Dickens and Ternan experienced together and Dickens' successful efforts to ensure that Ternan did not appear in any of the press accounts of the accident. The Ternan relationship plays a much smaller part in Ackroyd's biography and he concludes 'There can be no certainties here ... Nevertheless we are not talking of any ordinary friendship between a "great man" and a young woman ...'. But he chooses not pursue the mystery of the friendship further.

▶ Tomalin and Ackroyd were both 'looking' for different things in their biographies. Tomalin was intent on sifting through Dickens' life in search of 'the invisible woman'; Ackroyd was focused on producing a broader picture of Dickens and his life. In what ways do you think fixing on one aspect of someone's life – for example, one year in their life (as in *1599*, see Part 3, page 98), or in their relationship with one person (as in *The Invisible Woman*, page 112, above, or *The Silent Woman*, Part 3, page 93) – makes the biographer assess facts differently from a biographer who is taking a broader sweep?

Your own and other readers' interpretations

Just as biographers bring different perspectives to the lives they are writing about so the reader's response to different forms of life writing will be coloured by their own experiences and knowledge.

Read the extract from *I Know Why The Caged Bird Sings* (Part 3, page 76).

- In what way does the first line set the tone for the prologue?

- Do the final two lines give the reader any expectation of the tone of what might follow?

- In what ways do you think historical knowledge of racial segregation (in America or elsewhere) would give you greater understanding of, or sympathy for, the book and its author?

- Angelou introduces colour several times in this extract. Do you find any of the descriptions surprising and, if so, why?

- Do you think someone from an ethnic minority might read this extract in a different way from someone who is part of an ethnic majority? Likewise, how differently might Jewish and non-Jewish readers read the extract by Primo Levi (Part 3, page 91) ?

It is likely that the literary biography that you may have studied as a group will have produced different reactions. Gender, age, race or simply preferences for a particular style may each affect the way someone reads and responds to a piece of life writing. Every response is legitimate, but the reader who returns to the text to analyse the language, historical context and use of sources will develop the deepest appreciation of the author's intent.

Assignments

1   Imagine you have been asked to write the biography of a living author such as Ian McEwan. Who would you like to interview about their work and the influences of their life on their literary output? What questions would you ask your interviewees?

2   Visit the home of, or somewhere that would have been familiar to, a famous writer. Write a description of what it is like now and then write a second description of how it would have been different in the author's day. Can you identify any ways in which the place influenced their writing?

3   Choose an author or poet whose work you do not enjoy and read a biography, autobiography, or collection of journals or letters about their life. Did the life writing change or confirm your view of them and their work?

4   Pick any autobiography of an author that you have studied in depth. Are there any gaps in their account or any questions you would like answered?

5   Read the journals an author produced while they were working on a particular novel, play or poem. What light does the diary shed on the way that the literary work took shape?

6   Re-read your favourite literary biography and keep a note of what the biography tells you of the social and political conditions in which the author lived. How important is this to your understanding of the author's life? Do you think the lives of some authors require a fuller explanation of the social and political background in which they lived than others? If so, why and in which instances?

7   What particular insight can letters written *by* an author provide that other sources might not? Which recipients do you think would provide the most revealing letters – for example, letters written to a lover, publisher, fan or a casual acquaintance?

8   Zadie Smith was asked to choose which author she would like to interview for *New Beginnings* (see page 101). Which author (alive or dead) would you most like to interview? What questions would you ask them?

6 | Resources

Chronology of biographical texts and writers discussed

c. 50–c. 125   Plutarch

c. 1393   Julian of Norwich *Sixteen Revelations of Divine Love* (description of visions)

c. 1420s   *Book of Margery Kempe* (autobiography)

1579   Sir Thomas North, translation of Plutarch's *The Lives of the Noble Grecians and Romans*

1640   Izaak Walton, biography of the poet John Donne

1651   Izaak Walton, biography of the provost of Eton, Sir Henry Wotton

1665   Izaak Walton, biography of the Elizabethan theologian, Richard Hooker

1696   John Aubrey *Miscellanies* (stories and folklore)

1670   Izaak Walton, biography of the poet George Herbert

1678   Izaak Walton, biography of Bishop Sanderson

1744   Samuel Johnson *An Account of the Life of Mr Richard Savage, Son of the Earl Rivers* (biography)

1750   Samuel Johnson *On the Dignity and Usefulness of Biography* (essay in *The Rambler*)

1755   Samuel Johnson *Dictionary*

1791   James Boswell *The Life of Samuel Johnson*

1798   William Godwin *Memoirs of the Author of a Vindication of the Rights of Woman* (biography of his wife, Mary Wollstonecraft)

1813   Percy Bysshe Shelley *Queen Mab* (poem); first selection of John Aubrey's *Brief Lives* (sketches of eminent people)

1818   Henry Austen 'Biographical Note' (preface to first edition of Jane Austen's *Northanger Abbey* and *Persuasion*)

1851   Thomas Carlyle *Life of Sterling* (biography)

1857   Elizabeth Gaskell *The Life of Charlotte Brontë* (biography)

1870   James Edward Austen-Leigh *A Memoir of Jane Austen* (first biography – by her nephew)

1872–4	John Forster *Dickens* (three-volume biography)
1881	Thomas Carlyle *Reminiscences*
1885	First edition of *Dictionary of National Biography* (*DNB*)
1890	Sir Edmund Gosse *The Life of Philip Henry Gosse* (first biography of his father)
1898	Second, bowdlerised, edition of John Aubrey's *Brief Lives*
1907	Sir Edmund Gosse *Father and Son*
1918	Giles Lytton Strachey *Eminent Victorians* (biographical essays on Cardinal Manning, Florence Nightingale, Thomas Arnold and General Gordon)
1921	Giles Lytton Strachey *Queen Victoria* (biography)
1928	Giles Lytton Strachey *Elizabeth and Essex: A Tragic History* (biography); Virginia Woolf *Orlando* (fictional biography)
1929	Virginia Woolf *A Room of One's Own* (autobiographical essay); Robert Graves *Goodbye to All That* (autobiography)
1933	Vera Brittain *Testament of Youth* (autobiography)
1940	Vera Brittain *Testament of Friendship* (autobiography)
1947	Primo Levi *If This is a Man* (Holocaust memoir published in Italy)
1952	Anne Frank *The Diary of a Young Girl*; Doris Lessing *Martha Quest* (novel)
1953	Leonard Woolf (editor) *A Writer's Diary* (Virginia Woolf's diary)
1957	Vera Brittain *Testament of Experience* (autobiography)
1958	Truman Capote *Breakfast at Tiffany's* (novella)
1959	Laurie Lee *Cider with Rosie* (autobiography/memoir)
1960	Primo Levi *If This is a Man* (first UK translation); Sylvia Plath *The Colossus* (poetry); Anne Sexton *To Bedlam and Part Way Back* (poetry)
1963	Sylvia Plath *The Bell Jar* (novel)
1965	Sylvia Plath *Ariel* (poetry)
1966	Truman Capote *In Cold Blood* ('non-fiction novel'); Anne Sexton *Live or Die* (poetry)
1967	Michael Holroyd *Lytton Strachey: The Unknown Years* (biography)

1968	Michael Holroyd *Lytton Strachey: The Years of Achievement* (biography); Joseph Randolph Ackerley *My Father and Myself*
1969	Laurie Lee *As I Walked Out One Midsummer Morning* (autobiography); Kurt Vonnegut *Slaughterhouse Five*
1970	Maya Angelou *I Know Why the Caged Bird Sings* (autobiography)
1974	Richard Holmes *Shelley: The Pursuit* (biography); Claire Tomalin *The Life and Death of Mary Wollstonecraft* (biography)
1975–80	Nigel Nicolson and Joanne Trautmann (editors) *The Letters of Virginia Woolf*
1975	A. Plath (editor) *Letters Home*
1977–84	Ann Olivier Bell and Andrew McNeillie (editors) *The Diary of Virginia Woolf*
1982	Ted Hughes (editor) *The Journals of Sylvia Plath*; Janet Frame *To The Is-Land* (autobiography); Thomas Keneally *Schindler's Ark*
1983	Peter Ackroyd *The Last Testament of Oscar Wilde* (novel)
1984	J.G. Ballard *Empire of the Sun;* Louise DeSalvo and Mitchell Leaska (editors) *The Letters of Vita Sackville-West to Virginia Woolf*; Janet Frame *An Angel At My Table*
1985	Richard Holmes *Footsteps: Adventures of a Romantic Biographer* (biographical essays); Peter Ackroyd *Hawksmoor* (novel); Primo Levi *The Periodic Table* (UK translation of autobiographical essays)
1987	Claire Tomalin *Katherine Mansfield: A Secret Life* (biography)
1988	Michael Holroyd *Bernard Shaw Volume 1: The Search for Love, 1856–1898;* Margaret Forster *Elizabeth Barrett Browning: A Biography*
1989	Richard Holmes *Coleridge: Early Visions* (biography); Michael Holroyd *Bernard Shaw Volume 2: The Pursuit of Power, 1898–1918;* Anne Stevenson *Bitter Fame* (biography of Sylvia Plath)
1990	Peter Ackroyd *Dickens* (biography); Claire Tomalin *The Invisible Woman: The Story of Nelly Ternan and Charles Dickens* (biography)
1991	Michael Holroyd *Bernard Shaw Volume 3: The Lure of Fantasy, 1918–1950;* Diane Wood Middlebrook *Anne Sexton: A Biography*
1992	Michael Holroyd *Bernard Shaw Volume 4: The Last Laugh, 1950–1991;* Muriel Spark *Curriculum Vitae*; Brian Keenan *An Evil Cradling*

1993	Richard Holmes *Dr Johnson and Mr Savage* (biography); Blake Morrison *And When Did You Last See Your Father?*; Margaret Forster *Daphne Du Maurier* (biography)
1994	Claire Tomalin *Mrs Jordan's Profession* (biography); Janet Malcolm *The Silent Woman, Sylvia Plath & Ted Hughes*; Doris Lessing *Under My Skin* (autobiography)
1995	Margaret Forster *Hidden Lives: A Family Memoir;* Mark Bostridge and Paul Berry *Vera Brittain: A Life* (biography)
1996	Hermione Lee *Virginia Woolf: A Biography*; Frank McCourt *Angela's Ashes* (novel)
1997	Claire Tomalin *Jane Austen: A Life*; David Nokes *Jane Austen*; Doris Lessing *Walking in the Shade: Volume II of My Autobiography 1949–1962*
1998	Richard Holmes *Coleridge: Darker Reflections* (biography); Ted Hughes *Birthday Letters* (poetry); Margaret Forster *Precious Lives* (memoir); Kathryn Hughes *George Eliot: The Last Victorian*; Paul Theroux *Sir Vidia's Shadow: A Friendship Across Five Continents*; John Bayley *Iris* (memoir)
1999	Diana Souhami *Gertrude and Alice: Gertrude Stein and Alice B. Toklas*
2000	Lorna Sage *Bad Blood: A Memoir*
2001	Peter Conradi *Iris Murdoch: A Life*; Diana Souhami *Selkirk's Island*
2002	Michael Holroyd *Works on Paper: The Craft of Biography and Autobiography* (essays and articles on biography and writing); Carole Angier *The Double Bond: Primo Levi, A Biography*; Ian Thomson *Primo Levi* (biography); Blake Morrison *Things My Mother Never Told Me* (memoir); Claire Tomalin *Samuel Pepys: The Unequalled Self*
2003	Nigel Slater *Toast, The Story of a Boy's Hunger* (memoir); Margaret Forster *Diary of an Ordinary Woman: A Novel*; A.N. Wilson *Iris Murdoch as I Knew Her* (memoir)
2005	Hermione Lee *Body Parts: Essays on Life Writing*; Kathryn Hughes *The Short Life and Long Times of Mrs Beeton*; James Shapiro *1599: A Year in the Life of William Shakespeare*; Allan Bennett *Untold Stories* (memoir)

2006	Claire Tomalin *Thomas Hardy: The Time-torn Man*; Byron Rogers *The Man Who Went Into the West: The Life of R.S. Thomas*; Richard Davenport-Hines *A Night at the Majestic*
2007	*Letters of Ted Hughes*; Charles Nicholl *The Lodger: Shakespeare on Silver Street* (biography); Alison Light *Mrs Woolf and the Servants, The Hidden Heart of Domestic Service;* Charlotte Mosley (editor) *Mitfords: Letters Between Six Sisters*
2008	Patrick French *The World Is What It Is: The Authorized Biography of V.S. Naipaul*; J.G. Ballard *Miracles of Life: Shanghai to Shepperton*; Doris Lessing *Alfred and Emily*

Further reading

Books by and about individual authors are listed in the Chronology above.

Paula R. Backscheider *Reflections on Biography* (Oxford University Press, 2001)
Takes a critical approach to life writing and how the choices biographers make can have a far-reaching impact on the book they produce.

Mark Bostridge, ed. *Lives for Sale, Biographers' Tales* (Continuum, 2004)
A fascinating collection of essays on the practice of biography including many by leading literary biographers such as Kathryn Hughes, Michael Holroyd, Hermione Lee, Claire Tomalin and Jenny Uglow.

Bill Buford, ed. *Granta: Biography 41* (Penguin Books / Granta, 1992)
A special edition of the magazine looks at how a writer tells the story of a life, with contributions from Andrew Motion, Gabriel Garcia Marquez, Richard Holmes and Lorna Sage.

Margaret Drabble, ed. *The Oxford Companion to English Literature* (revised edition, Oxford University Press, 2006)
A general reference guide to individual authors, movements and genres from the medieval period to the present.

Richard Holmes *Footsteps: Adventures of a Romantic Biographer* (Flamingo, 1995)
Originally published in 1985 after completing his first major biography, *Shelley The Pursuit* (1974), *Footsteps* provides an insight into what it means to be a biographer.

Michael Holroyd *Works on Paper: The Craft of Biography and Autobiography Writing* (Little, Brown, 2002)
A witty collection of essays about all types of life writing by the author of books on subjects including George Bernard Shaw and Lytton Strachey.

Hermione Lee *Body Parts: Essays on Life-writing* (Chatto and Windus, 2005)
The biographer of Virginia Woolf, Edith Wharton, Willa Cather and others examines approaches to life writing in a series of reviews and essays.

Janet Malcolm *The Silent Woman, Sylvia Plath & Ted Hughes* (Granta, 2005)
Ostensibly about the reputation of a literary couple, this book takes a searching look at the practice and ethics of biography.

Phyllis Rose, ed. *The Penguin Book of Women's Lives* (Penguin, 1995)
A wide range of life writing by women from around the world.

C.K. Stead *The Writer at Work* (Otago University Press, 2000)
A selection of essays by a distinguished New Zealand writer and critic that mix literary criticism with autobiography.

Vendela Vida, ed. *Believer Book of Writers Talking to Writers* (Believer Books, 2005)
Writers such as Zadie Smith and David Eggars talk to fellow authors including Ian McEwan, Joan Didion, John Banville, Tom Stoppard and Janet Malcolm.

Websites

www.contemporarywriters.com/authors
The British Council's database provides biographies, bibliographies and critical reviews of some of the UK and Commonwealth's most important living writers and some authors from the Republic of Ireland.

www.oxforddnb.com
The Oxford Dictionary of National Biography
An illustrated collection of over 56,521 specially commissioned biographies of the men and women from around the world who shaped all aspects of Britain's past.

www.nationalarchives.gov.uk
This website offers advice about where to find many kinds of documents, some of which are available online.

nobelprize.org/nobel_prizes/literature/laureates
This website includes articles about writers who have won the Nobel Prize.

topics.nytimes.com/top/features/books/bookreviews/index.html
A free collection of book reviews published in *The New York Times* since 1981.

Glossary

Allusion an indirect reference, generally to a person, place or literary work, which enriches the reading context by calling up a set of associations.

Authorised a biography is said to be authorised if the subject or their family has given their approval and have usually seen the manuscript before it is published.

Bloomsbury Group the name given to the group of friends who originally met in the home of Virginia Woolf and her sister, Vanessa Bell when they were unmarried and lived in Gordon Square, Bloomsbury in London. The group included influential thinkers and writers such as the economist John Maynard Keynes, biographer Lytton Strachey and novelist E.M. Forster. Many of its members aimed to overthrow the artistic limitations of the Victorian age.

Bowdlerised when parts of a piece of writing that might be seen as indecent are 'cleaned up' to protect the reader. Dr Thomas Bowdler (1754–1825) gave his name to this term after he produced a sanitised version of Shakespeare's plays.

Freudian referring to the beliefs of Sigmund Freud (1856–1939), generally held to be the creator of psychoanalysis, he placed considerable emphasis on the unconscious mind and the influence of childhood on the adult character.

Genre although genre is often used loosely to refer to prose, poetry and drama as the three main forms of literary writing, it has a more specific meaning. Types of writing such as the Gothic novel, war poetry, biography, diaries and letters can be described as genres, identifying a group of texts that share key features of form, theme or approach.

Hagiography originally the writing of the lives of saints, this has come to mean a biography that idealises its subject.

Imagery generally, any figurative, non-literal language – including poetic devices such as metaphors and similes – aimed at evoking pictorial images in the mind of the reader or listener.

Literary biography the study of the life of a writer or poet which examines the influence of their life on their work.

Modernism the dominant movement of thought and art (literature, music, painting, architecture, etc.) in the earlier 20th century. Originally a reaction against established 19th century (Romantic / Victorian) forms and attitudes, it was experimental not conservative, international, intellectual and metropolitan not rural and romantic, responding to the impact of the new technological age. Writers such as D.H. Lawrence, Virginia Woolf and T.S. Eliot were at the centre of literary Modernism in Britain during the First World War (1914–1918) and the 1920s.

Mood the emotional atmosphere created in a literary work. The creation of mood frequently depends on the author's use of language.

Narrative / narrator literally the sequential telling of an event or story; in prose (especially fiction) and often in poetry, it is important to describe the narrative structure of a text (the way the story / argument / situation, etc. is organised and presented) and to identify the narrative voice and / or the narrative perspective being adopted. Prose, diaries, letters, etc. may contain narrative; a novel will have a narrator, who may be one of the characters (or the hero / heroine) or the author.

Primary source a source that was produced at the time, for example an original document such as a letter or an account of an event.

Pseudonym a pen name, an assumed name used for writing, often in order to hide an author's true identity.

Restoration the return of the monarchy to England following the Civil War and marked by the start of the reign of Charles II (1660).

Rhetorical question a question asked for dramatic purposes and to which no answer is expected.

Romantic Movement from about 1780 to 1848, the move towards imaginative spontaneity expressed by the individual and away from classical objectivity and restraint.

Tone an author's manner of expression. It generally conveys emotional attitudes and in a literary work depends on word choice. So, for example, a writer's tone might be serious, sarcastic or humorous.

Tradition (s) the conventions, developed over a long period, which characterise a way of thinking about particular topics or a way of writing in a given form. For example, we might speak of the poetic tradition, suggesting (among other things) verse with regular rhyme and meter.

Vernacular ordinary speech, especially the actual language or way of speaking of a particular group in a specific geographical area, rather than a 'learned' language such as Latin or Ancient Greek.

Index

Acknowledgements

The authors and publishers acknowledge the following sources of copyright material and are grateful for the permissions granted. While every effort has been made, it has not always been possible to identify the sources of all the material used, or to trace all copyright holders. If any omissions are brought to our notice, we will be happy to include the appropriate acknowledgements on reprinting.

pp.13, 63, 98–101: *1599, A Year in the Life of William Shakespeare* by James Shapiro, published by Faber and Faber Ltd. Copyright © 2005 by James Shapiro. Reprinted with permission of HarperCollins Publishers; pp.24, 103: Letter 'March 14, 1927', excerpt from 'September 20, 1927' *The Diary of Virginia Woolf, Volume III: 1925–1930* by Virginia Woolf. Copyright © 1980 by Quentin Bell and Angelica Garnett, reprinted by permission of Houghton Mifflin Harcourt Publishing Company. Excerpt from 'Wednesday 28 November 1928' in *The Diary of Virginia Woolf, Volume II: 1920–1924*. Copyright © 1978 by Quentin Bell and Angelica Garnett, reprinted by permission of Houghton Mifflin Harcourt Publishing Company. Used by permission of The Random House Group Ltd; p.25: *The Letters of Vita Sackville-West to Virginia Woolf* Reproduced with permission of Curtis Brown Group Ltd, London on behalf of the Estate of Vita Sackville-West. Copyright © The Estate of Vita Sackville-West 1984. Used by permission of The Society of Authors as the literary representative of the Estate of Virginia Woolf; p.29: *The Diary of a Young Girl: The Definitive Edition* by Anne Frank, edited by Otto Frank and Mirjam Pressler, translated by Susan Massotty (Viking, 1997). Copyright © The Anne Frank-Fonds, Basel, Switzerland, 1991. English translation copyright © Doubleday a division of Bantam Doubleday Dell Publishing Group Inc, 1995. Reproduced by permission of Penguin Books Ltd. Used by permission of Doubleday, a division of Random House, Inc.; p.30, 41, 30: Excerpts from articles 'Portrait of a Writer: Truman Capote' (*The New York Times*, 8/28/1984 © 1984 The New York Times) and 'Books of the Times; Surviving Auschwitz, Surrendering to Despair' (*The New York Times*, 11/8/2003 © 2003 The New York Times). All rights reserved. Used by permission and protected by the Copyright Laws of the United States. The printing, copying, redistribution or retransmission of the Material without express written permission is prohibited; p.32: *Nella Last's War, the Second World War Diaries of Housewife 49* Reproduced with permission of Curtis Brown Group Ltd, London on behalf of the Trustees of the Mass Observation Archive. Copyright © The Trustees of the Mass Observation Archive; p.34: *The Journals of Sylvia Plath*, edited by Ted Hughes, published by Faber and Faber Ltd. Copyright © 1982 by Ted Hughes as Executor of the Estate of Sylvia Plath. Used by permission of Doubleday, a division of Random House, Inc.; p.35: 'Visit' from *Birthday Letters* by Ted Hughes and excerpt from *Letters of Ted Hughes* (ed. Christopher Reid), published by Faber and Faber Ltd; p.40: Quote from article 'Wealthy Farmer, 3 of Family Slain' by Truman Capote (16 November 1959, published in *The New York Times*). Copyright © United Press International, Inc.; p.41: Quote by Peter Ackroyd from article 'London Calling' by John O'Mahony, *Guardian*, 3 July 2004; pp. 59–60, 75–76, 113–114: *Dickens* by Peter Ackroyd, published by Sinclair-Stevenson/Vintage. Reprinted by permission of The Random House Group Ltd; p.46: *Footsteps, Adventures of a Romantic Biographer* by Richard Holmes reprinted by permission of HarperCollins Publishers Ltd. Copyright © Richard Holmes, 1985; p.56, 92–93: *Mrs Woolf and the Servants* by Alison Light (Fig Tree 2007, Penguin Books 2008). Copyright © Alison Light, 2007. Reproduced by permission of Penguin Books Ltd; pp.62, 109: Excerpts from articles from *The Times* by permission of NI Syndication; p.67: *Terry Castle stands by Jane Austin review*. Stanford News Service press release (16 August 1995). © Stanford University. All rights reserved. Stanford, CA 94305; p.71: Quote by Ian McEwan from article 'Enduring Fame' by Aida Edermariam. Copyright © Guardian News & Media Ltd 2007; pp.76–78: *I Know Why the Caged Bird Sings* by Maya Angelou, published by Little, Brown Book Group. Copyright © 1969 and renewed 1997 by Maya Angelou. Used by permission of Random House, Inc.; pp.80–82: *Empire of the Sun* and *Miracles of Life* by J.G. Ballard, published by HarperCollins Publishers Ltd. Copyright © J.G. Ballard, 1984 and 2008; pp.82–86: Excerpts from *Testament of Youth* by Vera Brittain (1933) and from *Letters from a Lost Generation. First World War Letters of Vera Brittain and Four Friends*, edited by Alan Bishop and Mark Bostridge (1998), are included by permission of Mark Bostridge and Timothy Brittain-Catlin, Literary Executors for the Vera Brittain Estate 1970; pp.88–91: *Alfred and Emily* by Doris Lessing, reprinted by kind permission of HarperCollins Publishing Ltd. and Jonathan Clowes Ltd., London, on behalf of Doris Lessing. Copyright © Doris Lessing 2008; pp.91–92: *If This is a Man* by Primo Levi, published by Bodley Head. Reprinted by permission of The Random House Group Ltd and Guilio Einaudi editore S. p.A.; pp.93–96: *The Silent Woman* by Janet Malcolm published by Pan Macmillan. Copyright © Janet Malcolm, 2005; p.97: 'Morning Song' from *Ariel* by Sylvia Plath. Copyright © 1961 by Ted Hughes. Reprinted by permission of HarperCollins Publishers. Published by Faber and Faber Ltd; pp.101–103: Excerpt from *The Believer Book of Writers Talking to Writers*, Believer Books, 2005. Used by permission of A.P. Watt Ltd on behalf of Zadie Smith. Copyright © Ian McEwan. Reproduced by permission of the author c/o Rogers, Coleridge & White Ltd., 20 Powis Mews, London W11 1JN; p.108: Quote from article by Blake Morrison. Copyright © Guardian News & Media Ltd 2008

WRITING LIVES